# FRANKLIN *and* ELEANOR
# *in* NEW YORK

*Also by* MICHAEL J. BURGESS

*Rose Kryzak and the Senior Action Movement in New York*

*A Long Shot to Glory : How Lake Placid Saved
the Winter Olympics and Restored the Nation's Pride*

*Keeper of the Olympic Flame: Lake Placid's
Jack Shea vs. Avery Brundage and the Nazi Olympics.*

# FRANKLIN *and* ELEANOR *in* NEW YORK

*The Progressive Agenda for Security and
Prosperity That Became the New Deal*

MICHAEL J. BURGESS

# TABLE OF CONTENTS

# PREFACE

FRANKLIN AND ELEANOR ROOSEVELT changed America with a government on the side of the people that put Americans back to work and inspired confidence that the nation could overcome the Great Depression. This is the story of their progressive legacy that began when Franklin Roosevelt was Governor of New York as the Great Depression struck and upended life for most Americans. It was during the era of Prohibition, speakeasies, flappers and the new medium of radio in the Roaring Twenties. It was a time when, as Governor, Roosevelt tried new programs that became the New Deal that transformed America. His warm, easily relatable, voice heard on the radio for the first time created a bond of trust with the public that inspired confidence at a time of great fear.

Roosevelt's New Deal in the White House was the time when government began to play a major role in insuring the economic security of Americans. That commitment began in Albany as the Great Depression crushed the world economy and sent fear into everyday life. Roosevelt's programs at the state level as the Depression began became the basis for much of the New Deal. He committed to an activist government of relief, employment programs, pensions for older adults, regulation of banks and private markets and guarantees of labor rights. The programs fundamentally changed the relationship of the government with its citizens. This book discusses those programs and how FDR brought his key advisors from Albany to Washington who implemented the historic progressive achievements of the New Deal in the White House.

This book also discusses Roosevelt's commitment to human rights and faith in democracy. He enunciated those so clearly in 1941 outlining his famous Four Freedoms. While the nation experienced his faith during the Depression and World War II when totalitarian regimes tried to conquer the world, Roosevelt had always had a idealistic faith in the ability of citizens to be self-governing. He sought often to educate the public about the issues and functions of government.

Both Franklin as President and then Eleanor after his death pushed for international peace and human rights across the globe through their commitment to the United Nations and Eleanor's connection to the emerging civil rights movement with Rosa Parks and Martin Luther King and others before her death.

There have been many detailed, wonderful biographies and historical books about the lives of Franklin and Eleanor Roosevelt and their time in the White House. In fact, the Roosevelt story has been told many times by well known, skilled historians. This book is not a biography about Franklin and Eleanor Roosevelt or a documentary of their White House years. However, extensive quotes from speeches and comments by Franklin and Eleanor Roosevelt are included to provide a sense of their thoughts in their own words.

This book is a story focusing mostly on their time in Albany during FDR's governorship, to look at those days through our modern eyes and follow the impact on his presidency and on American government in the decades that followed. Highlights of his government activities and travels around the state during his time as Governor are detailed along with some little known personal stories about the Roosevelts' lives in Albany. The personal struggles Roosevelt had in walking and getting places are described along with his determination and spirit to lead a full life.

There are frequent references to other historic events that are of great interest in current times. The epidemics of the Spanish flu, polio and other contagious diseases that struck Roosevelt are noted because the fragility of public health then was not feared again for decades until recently.

Roosevelt first spent time in Albany in 1911-13 when he was a State Senator and then they lived at the Executive Mansion when he served as Governor in 1929-33. Though the book's main focus is on those years, it is important to put that era in context and discuss how Franklin Roosevelt got to the Executive Mansion in Albany. The earlier chapters of the book briefly sketch those early years of Franklin and Eleanor, their relationship with President Theodore Roosevelt, who was Eleanor's uncle and Franklin's cousin. Then, Roosevelt's election to the New York State Legislature in the Progressive era as a reformer is discussed along with his emergence on the national political stage at the Democratic nominee for Vice President in 1920.

His early political years are followed by the event that forever changed his life when he contracted polio at the family summer home at Campobello Island, New Brunswick, off the coast of Maine. He was partially paralyzed but able to regain physical health through extensive therapy at Warm Springs, Georgia. He re-emerged in the political world and by 1928, he re-entered politics when he was elected Governor of New York.

The last sections of the book discuss the impact and legacy of the New Deal. The programs, policies and ideals of the Roosevelts have shaped every presidential administration in the eight decades that have followed and their ideals have continued to influence government in Albany and Washington. Their legacy has endured and become valued again during the Great Recession, the global coronavirus pandemic and resulting social and economic crises of the 21st century.

*Governor Franklin D. Roosevelt addressing the New York State Legislature in the Assembly Chamber, Albany, 1929*

# INTRODUCTION

THE STORY OF THE WEALTHY ROOSEVELT FAMILY is an American epic to rival a fictional drama like Downton Abbey in the same era early in the twentieth century in England.  The Hyde Park estate where Franklin Roosevelt grew up was like an English country manor with maids, cooks, farm hands and nurses and governesses.  Franklin and Eleanor Roosevelt were born in the same extended family in the 1880s to great wealth.  He was the handsome, privileged son of James and Sara Roosevelt who guided him to be a self-confident young man, eager to make his mark in public affairs.

His father, James, was a wealthy Vice President of the Delaware and Hudson Railroad and Supervisor of the Town of Hyde Park.  Though James never sought higher office he was a politically connected Democrat and a supporter and friend of New York Governor and President Grover Cleveland.  There was a story that James introduced his five year old son, Franklin, to Cleveland who said to him, "My little man, I am making a strange wish for you. It is that you may never be president of the United States."

James Roosevelt was related to the original Dutch families in the United States including the Livingstones and the Schuylers.  He graduated from Union College in Schenectady in 1847.  James married his second cousin, Rebecca Howland, and had a son James who was known as "Rosey." After Rebecca died in 1876, he married Franklin's mother.

1

Sara Delano traced her roots to the Mayflower and also came from a family of great wealth. Her father, Warren Delano, Jr. made a fortune smuggling illegal opium into China in the mid-1800s. She grew up in Newburgh, New York and spent three years in Hong Kong. She was also related to the Astor family, one of the wealthiest of the era who owned a palatial mansion nearby.

The Roosevelts lived at their estate in Hyde Park which they called Springwood. Prominent neighbors who were even wealthier in the Hudson Valley included the Vanderbilts as well as the Astors. "Rosey" Roosevelt was married to one of the daughters of William Backhouse Astor.

As David Kennedy writes in *Freedom from Fear,* "The patrician father and doting mother conferred on their only son the priceless endowment of an unshakable sense of self worth. They also nurtured in him a robust social conscience." He went to Groton "in the heyday of the Social Gospel movement, the Rev. Endicott Peabody instilled in his young charges the lessons of Christian duty and the ethic of public service." He had a great interest in the Navy and started collecting naval items as a hobby at a young age.

When James Roosevelt died in 1900, Franklin and Sara's world was turned upside down. Franklin's bond with his mother as her only son grew ever stronger. She inherited the family fortune and was able to support him in all his schooling and interests. Throughout his later life in politics, she also provided financial support when he needed it. Franklin went to Groton prep school and then to Harvard and earned a law degree though he was much more interested in political life than practicing law.

The woman we know in history as Eleanor Roosevelt had a difficult childhood, deprived of affection and nurturing and with both parents dead before she was a teenager. She was a fifth cousin to Franklin, a shy, young woman lacking self-confidence. Her mother considered her ugly and called her "granny" as a child. She died of diphtheria when Eleanor was just eight years old. Her father, Elliott, was an alcoholic who attempted suicide. Her grandmother Hall decided it would be best if she could be sent to a boarding school in England called Allenswood. There she came under the steady nurturing of Madame Marie Silvestre who built her confidence as she became a young woman between the ages of 15 and 18 from 1899-1902.

It was there she began to flower. She credited Mme. Silvestre for developing her self-esteem and widening her horizons as she took her on trips through Europe and exposed her to the wider world of knowledge. Stephen Cope wrote in his book, *Soul Friends,* "Eleanor Roosevelt matured into one of the most powerful and impressive women of her era. Indeed, during World War II she became the virtual mother of the country - a container for the suffering and the high aspirations of an entire nation."

When she returned home she began teaching exercise and dancing to children of Italian and Jewish immigrants at the Rivington Settlement House in New York. Eleanor and Franklin saw each other at family events and fell in love despite Sara Roosevelt's disapproval. Sara felt Eleanor was not good enough for him and she tried to dissuade him from marrying her. Franklin found her a serious and intelligent young woman.

Eleanor's uncle and Franklin's cousin was Theodore Roosevelt who had been elected to the New York State Legislature and then served as Assistant Secretary of the Navy under President McKinley. He was elected Governor of New York in 1898 and then Vice President in 1900 on the Republican ticket with William McKinley.

Less than a year later he was President when McKinley was assassinated, after being shot in Buffalo and then lingered for a couple months before dying in September 1901. Teddy was elected President in his own right in 1904 and Franklin and Eleanor attended Teddy's inauguration in Washington in January 1905. Two months later on

March 17, 1905, it was Teddy as President of the United States who gave away Eleanor when she married Franklin. "I feel as if she is my own daughter," Teddy said. He would be a close uncle to Eleanor and would become a political mentor for Franklin in the years to come.

After they were married, Franklin's mother Sara, made sure she was still a close part of his life by financing a double townhouse at East 65th Street in New York. She would live on one side and Franklin and Eleanor on the other side. For years, Eleanor would feel that she never really had her own home. She remarked that it wasn't until Franklin built the Val-Kill cottage for her at the Hyde Park estate that she had her own place.

A casual observer of American history might think that Theodore and Franklin Roosevelt were in two different eras. They were born 24 years apart and they did not share the same party and were indeed from two different wings of the Roosevelt family in Hyde Park and Oyster Bay on Long Island. Franklin, though not in the same political party, literally followed in Teddy's footsteps by occupying the same offices in the New York State Legislature, Assistant Secretary of the Navy, Governor and President. He had entered the political world greatly influenced by his cousin and by the Progressive Era of which Teddy was a champion and central figure as President in the first decade of the twentieth century.

Despite all of his privileges, Franklin was beset with serious illnesses, including the one that forever changed his life when he contracted polio at the age of 39 and was never able to walk unaided again. That experience and his determination to overcome it and lead a full life, never complaining and always looking on the bright side, made him a more compassionate leader. After having been nominated for Vice President on the 1920 Democratic ticket with James Cox, he had to withdraw from public life for several years until he had regained enough strength to lead a life as normal as possible. In 1928 he still wanted to spend more time gaining strength but he agreed reluctantly to run for

Governor of New York. Some thought Roosevelt was just put into the Governor's mansion by Al Smith and that he had no clear convictions. Years later, Louis Lefkowitz who was an Assemblyman during FDR's governorship and later became New York State Attorney General stated, "He knew exactly what he wanted and was determined to get it."

Roosevelt came into the Governor's office at a time marked by great change. It was the end of the Roaring Twenties which had brought unprecedented prosperity to America after World War I. The 1920s can be viewed in a sense as the beginning of modern political history. It was an era that would usher in mass communications for the first time as radios became widely available, enabling society to be better connected including citizens with their political leaders. The congenial and warm, relatable manner of Franklin Roosevelt enabled him to master the radio to promote his political agenda and campaigns.

It was also the era of Prohibition. The decade would end with the Great Depression, a devastating economic calamity for America with millions unemployed and destitute. It set off a questioning of capitalism and social upheavals causing in Roosevelt's view the greatest crisis at that time since the 60s - the 1860s and the Civil War.

When he became Governor in 1929 New York State was the largest state in the country with 12 million residents. It had 45 electoral votes, giving it an outsized influence in national politics. New York City was the largest and most dominant city in the country. His reaction to the Depression with bold economic policies to put people back to work and his familiar name and relation to a previous President Roosevelt elevated him as the leading candidate for the Presidency in 1932.

For those who have worked in and around state government in more recent years, it is amazing that over 90 years ago FDR was dealing with many of the same issues about the process of governing.

He complained about decisions made by a small group of legislative leaders and budget bills presented at the last minute before legislators had a chance to read them. He complained about excessive partisanship and the power of private interests who were able to contribute large campaign contributions to influence elections. He complained about the costs of local government and high taxes. He battled in court with a Republican controlled legislature about the power of the Governor in making budgetary decisions.

Business interests fought his plans to reduce the workweek to 48 hours fearing business would leave the state. He said "give credit to the legislature for acting on a very large percentage of measures during the final two weeks, even though it was the same old story of sitting here in Albany month after month without action, while a small group of leaders were trying to make up their minds what to do."

In a radio address in April 1930 after the Legislature had acted on the budget, he complained, "The Legislature had only passed one bill in three months and then, it adjourned at 2:00 in the morning after a hectic two weeks. It is all very well to say that this is the usual method of procedure. That is perfectly true, but it does not get away from the fact that the rank and file of senators and assemblymen have no opportunity to know anything about or study the great majority of bills that actually pass or are defeated."

So much in his role as Governor is similar to the role today in that Governors are pre-occupied with many of the same major issues because state agencies run or fund state run prisons and institutions, public schools, criminal justice, health care, taxes.

Even though the processes were similar, it is stunning to read about how people in need were viewed in those days and the language that was used. He talked about "wards of the state," the "cripples" "morons" and the "insane" and not wanting people to be "on the dole."

Of course there have been many changes in the operation of state government. In 1931 the Alfred E. Smith State Office Building was built in Albany and all of state government was contained in the the

State Education Building, the Smith building and a few others. The Governor actually lived in the Governor's Executive Mansion on Eagle Street. The legislators all met and worked in the Capitol building. Only a half century later after Nelson Rockefeller built the Empire State Plaza did they move into their own building with their own office suites.

Franklin and Eleanor Roosevelt often traveled the state in those simpler times. FDR liked to drive around the state and often Eleanor would travel with him and be his eyes and ears to report on what she saw on her inspections of state facilities and other sites.

The legacy of Franklin Roosevelt and the era that he and Al Smith dominated one hundred years ago in New York created the modern state government, paving the way for future governors like Nelson Rockefeller who greatly expanded public services and buildings. 50 years after FDR served in Albany Governor Mario Cuomo was viewed as the most eloquent disciple and advocate of Roosevelt's progressive view that government can be a positive instrument to make life better for average citizens.

Nationally, the New Deal that FDR and the Democratic Congress enacted after he went to the White House has become permanently institutionalized with programs that built a social safety net that has been expanded over the years to later include Medicare, Medicaid, the Americans with Disabilities Act, and the Affordable Care Act.

The New Deal remained controversial and Republicans and conservatives continually tried to dismantle it or privatize programs like Social Security for decades and this effort still goes on.

The New Deal was a pragmatic and immediate response to the failures of American capitalism and the speculation on Wall Street which produced the Great Depression. It came at a time when many democracies were still reacting to the overthrow of the Russian government at the end of World War I and the establishment of a Marxist-Communist government. This opposition to Communism would be a defining feature of American society in the years following both world wars. In this country, socialism never took a Communist form as socialists like Norman Thomas pushed for more government control of key sectors of the economy, specifically those which affected the basic economic needs of citizens. They never sought to create a dictatorship. In fact, Thomas and others felt that the New Deal did not go far enough and the success of the New Deal took a lot of the political momentum from the socialist movement.

## Eleanor

The story and personal relationship of Franklin and Eleanor Roosevelt is a complicated one. It was a relationship that could have ended since Eleanor offered Franklin the opportunity to divorce her. Franklin was a man who attracted women and had close relationships and affairs with more than one. In the postwar years, Eleanor found letters in his coat pocket to Lucy Mercer who had been her assistant. To get a divorce would have ended Franklin's political career in those days. He promised never to see Lucy Mercer again and he and Eleanor stayed together, seemingly with an agreement to allow each freedom in their private friendships with others. Their romantic relationship changed for good though.

In the years to come, both Franklin and Eleanor would pursue close relationships with other persons. For Franklin it was being around female company like his cousin Daisy Suckley, his secretary Missy Le-Hand or during World War II with the exiled Princess Martha of Norway. For Eleanor it was New York State state trooper Earl Miller who was assigned to protect and accompany her. She enjoyed having fun with him when she was the state's First Lady. Later, she would have a close relationship and rumored to be a romantic one with reporter

Lorena Hickok. She also had a number of close feminist friends who were involved in suffragette, consumer and political causes including Marion Dickerman, Nancy Cook, Esther Lape and Elizabeth Read.

Eleanor supported Franklin in his personal struggles adjusting to polio and became his political partner standing in for him after he was stricken, hoping that he would be healthy enough to return to a public life in electoral politics. She became active in a number of civic and women's political organizations. She said that she was only doing so until he could resume his work, but she had found her calling in public affairs and serving people. She had evolved from being a shy, somewhat traditional, conservative wealthy woman to becoming a progressive activist in public affairs.

Their political relationship was based on a shared view of progressive politics and activist government to benefit the common person. He was the master politician and she was the advocate for the average citizen especially those in need; she sought to support his policies in her public roles and through her alliances with many people and causes she supported. She was indefatigable and viewed as overstepping her bounds by many in government agencies when he was President who felt she was pushing her own agenda. He admired her convictions and valued her advice because she was in touch with many people and organizations through her constant travels. Most often he agreed with her views and he tried to find the best way to gain the political support to enact some of her ideas. In her book *No Ordinary Time* Doris Kearns Goodwin wrote, "While Eleanor thought of what *should* be done, Franklin thought in terms of what *could* be done."

She would become even more formidable in her role as First Lady of the United States to become a controversial and historic figure, a legendary icon for civil rights and social justice. She had been not thrilled for herself when her husband ran and won the Presidency, but she used her role to champion the causes of those who were left out and without a voice, particularly women and African Americans. She had a strong empathy for underprivileged people and for civil rights and human rights and she was determined to use her role and proximity to power to advocate for social change. She never undercut the agenda of her husband but she was always advocating for action, which Franklin often supported or slowed her down.

She never pressed her differing views to make his public positions more difficult. Years later in her book *This I Remember* she talked about her advocacy with her husband, "Often people came to me to enlist his support for an idea. Although I might present the situation to him, I never urged on him a specific course of action, no matter how strongly I felt, because I realized he knew of factors in the picture as a whole of which I might be ignorant. I would do all I could for the people who came to me, short of stating what my husband might think or feel, and he never asked me to refrain from speaking my own mind."

She played that role especially in the White House, traveling around the country and the world. She flew with her friend, Amelia Earhart, and later with a Tuskegee Airman, took the dangerous Olympic bobsled run in Lake Placid and went with miners down mineshafts, visited a Japanese internment camp and American troops in wartime England. She was a serious minded person who could not easily relax and enjoy downtime like her husband but their political partnership had never been seen in America before. She was so persistent that he would joke that he prayed, "Dear God, make Eleanor tired."

After his death in office, she would leave the White House and embark on seventeen more years of life, serving in the United States delegation to the United Nations and playing the key role in the passage of the Universal Declaration of Human Rights adopted in 1948. She became the "First Lady of the World" as Harry Truman called her who set a standard for every one who came after her.

Exactly two weeks after FDR took the oath of office in Albany, Martin Luther King Jr. was born in Atlanta. Thirty years later he and Eleanor and King would become political allies as the civil rights movement was building to its climax in the 1960s. She believed not just in the ideal of equality in a democratic society, but as a moral imperative based on Biblical principles about the dignity of every person. She joined with African American leaders to fight for an anti-lynching law in the 1930s and even sat in the United States Senate gallery for several days when the bill was being discussed so that her presence was noted.

Elliott Roosevelt decided to write about his father and mother many years later in 1972 in his book *The Untold Story*, the Roosevelts of Hyde Park. He wanted to present a realistic view of who his parents were as people who "came to greatness through tremendous physical and mental anguish." He explained why he wrote of them years later: "Recently, I became increasingly perturbed over a twisting of facts which had led far too many people to regard Father as a cardboard puppet, manipulated by anyone with the urge to try, dependent on Mother for strength and wisdom. She, in turn, is looked upon as a latter-day Joan of Arc, incapable of error or sin. Neither portrait contains the faintest element of truth. " Mother, whose idolators are largely responsible for this mangling of the record of yesterday would have been among the first to acknowledge that."

## Franklin

Franklin Roosevelt was the most politically successful president who won four terms, lifted the nation out of the Great Depression and led the country to victory in World War II. He is pictured as the man with the smile and good humor, unflappable and unruffled by stress and crises. Before the age of 40, his political path seemed headed there. There is a temptation to view his rise and political success as inevitable given his wealth, his demeanor, good looks and last name. Like all famous people, he did not get there alone or without struggles. In fact, though he aspired to be President given his family's wealth and prominence Franklin Roosevelt's political ascension was never a clear trajectory to the White House. Despite his ambition early in life to follow in his cousin Theodore Roosevelt's footsteps to the White House, Franklin Roosevelt was in many ways a very long shot to reach that goal.

Though he was a charming, handsome young State Senator with the name Roosevelt, he had an affected style of speaking and was considered arrogant and self-absorbed and not a person of firm beliefs when he first came to Albany in 1911. He said in his own words, "I was an awful cuss." Later as Governor and President he was disliked by many on the left for in their view, having no firm convictions and those on the right for policies they viewed as socialist governmental intervention.

Roosevelt had to be a wily politician because he was trying to ascend to political leadership as a reformer in a Democratic Party controlled by Tammany Hall in the early years of the century. Sometimes this led people to feel that his positions shifted and his word couldn't be trusted.

Warren Moscow who covered Roosevelt for the *New York Times* during Roosevelt's Albany years said, "He was a dissimulator. He had this habit of nodding and saying, 'Yes, yes, yes,' as if he was agreeing with you, and all he was doing was saying he heard you." One colleague in the New York State Assembly was quoted saying that "If Franklin Roosevelt had an honest hair on his head, they would have to pull it out."

Professor Frank Friedel said that the conventional views on Roosevelt as Governor were colored - to his detriment - by New York City liberals irritated that he had not controlled the political club of Tammany Hall and by conservatives who saw him as "the Boy Scout Governor," with a big grin but not much behind it.

Walter Lippmann, the great newspaper columnist of the era said, Roosevelt was "an amiable man with many philanthropic impulses, but he is not the dangerous enemy of anything . . . for F.D.R. is no crusader. He is no tribune of the people. He is no enemy of entrenched privilege. He is a pleasant man who, without any important qualifications for the office, would very much like to be President."

His political career was nearly ended in 1921 when he suddenly contracted polio and was permanently "crippled" and would never walk again unaided. Even when it became apparent that he could still work and function in politics, he resisted running for Governor of New York in 1928 and thought for sure on election night he had lost in the Republican tide that swept over the country and state.

In 1932, many thought his nomination and election for President was assured but he was viewed by his opponents as not physically able to do the job and a man of not clear ideas and policies to confront the Depression. And, just three weeks before he took the oath of office as President he came within a few feet of receiving an assassin's bullet that missed him and killed the Mayor of Chicago.

How did such a man overcome so many obstacles not of his making and then succeed and corral the roiling political waters during the Depression when democracies abroad were becoming dictatorships on the left and the right of Communism and fascism? And, how even as President did he manage to succeed when many people at home were so desperate they seized state capitals, talked of revolution and thought the nation needed much more revolutionary change than the New Deal against the lords of Wall Street?

Franklin Roosevelt was a brilliant politician and a man with great charm, a "first class temperament." as he was called by Justice Oliver Wendell Holmes. His success as a politician and President of the United States was directly related to his temperament. His self-confidence radiated from his strong voice and his likability earned him the trust of the people. He spoke to them on the radio like he was sitting in their living rooms.

His positive attitude also was reflected in his pragmatism to try new approaches and ideas and above all, to take action to try to solve social and economic problems. Not only did he believe in trying but he also understood what was politically possible.

James McGregor Burns in his biography of FDR, *The Lion and the Fox*, noted these traits when he was Governor, "Above all, the governor possessed the indispensable quality of accepting the need for change, for new departures, for experiments. He recognized that government was not a bogy but an instrument for meeting the problems of change. And he had the capacity to learn. It was these things that made his governorship truly an apprenticeship in politics and statecraft."

Eleanor summed up his impact in his critical moment in history, "I have never known a man who gave one a greater sense of security. That was because I never heard him say there was a problem that he thought it was impossible for human beings to solve. He recognized the difficulties and often said that while he did not know the answer, he was completely confident that there was an answer...I never knew him to face life, or any problem that came up with fear and I have often wondered if that courageous attitude was not communicated to the people of the country. It may well be what helped them to pull themselves out of the depression in the first years of his administration as president."

# CHAPTER 1

## The Progressive Era and the Roosevelts

AFTER ECONOMIC PANICS IN THE 1890s caused major upheavals in the agricultural and industrial sectors a mass political movement rose up to challenge the control of the economy by corporate trusts. Muckraking journalists like Upton Sinclair wrote about the dangers of largely unregulated capitalism and its impact on working people. The fire at the Triangle Shirt factory in New York City in 1911 that killed scores in a locked warehouse exposed the callousness and social irresponsibility of factory owners and galvanized efforts to protect workers. The movement gained political support from important leaders including President Theodore Roosevelt who was nicknamed the "trust buster" because breaking up monopolies was a major focus of his presidency as he pushed 44 anti-trust actions.

The Progressive Era was defined by this surging movement demanding reform to challenge concentrations of power not only in the economic sector but also to reform the American political system. The movement blossomed in the late 1800s and early 1900s when women still did not have the right to vote and United States Senators were elected by state legislatures rather than directly by the voters. Campaigns to enact constitutional amendments to enact suffrage for women and direct elections of senators were major political goals of the Progressive era. Also, reformers wanted to challenge local political machines including Tammany Hall in New York City where a small group of people controlled decision-making on most aspects of political life and the administration of government agencies.

Despite being in different parties, Franklin Roosevelt shared the progressive political philosophy of an activist and more democratic government with his cousin Teddy. Franklin's political career would later follow a similar path of his cousin who served as Assistant Secretary of the Navy in 1897 before running and being elected Governor of New York in 1898. Then, Teddy was selected by William McKinley as his second Vice President in 1900. Fate intervened when McKinley was assassinated and Roosevelt became President in September 1900.

Roosevelt dominated that first decade of the twentieth century and won election when he ran as the incumbent in 1904. Teddy's administration was the Square Deal as he sought to stand up for average citizens against the wealthy who controlled the economy. He railed against an "unholy alliance" of corrupt business and corrupt politics.

Teddy decided not to seek re-election in 1908 and William Howard Taft won the White House as his hand picked successor. Dissatisfied with Taft, Teddy ran again for President in 1912 and when he didn't win the Republican nomination, he ran on the Progressive Party ticket, known as the "Bull Moose" Party. Franklin Roosevelt was supporting Democrat Woodrow Wilson in 1912 who defeated Teddy with Taft finishing third.

## Entering Public Life in Albany

The progressive political movement was still ascendant at the time 28 year old Franklin Roosevelt was offered a chance by local Democrats to seek public office as a State Assembly member from Dutchess County. It was a Democratic district and he was eager to run. The Democrat incumbent changed his mind about not running and Franklin was offered a chance instead to run for a State Senate district in the Hudson River Valley north of New York City that had consistently sent Republicans to Albany. Franklin was willing to run and he campaigned vigorously, connecting in person with many people as he drove around the district. He wanted to be the first candidate to campaign by automobile so he traveled in a new red Maxwell touring car at a time where the horse and buggy was still the main method of travel.

While some have said that Franklin Roosevelt was so pragmatic a politician that he didn't have a definite political philosophy, he was clearly a reformer supporting the Progressive movement. In his earliest speeches and public remarks, he expressed an idealistic vision of democracy that was controlled by the citizens not by party bosses. Roosevelt stressed his own independence in his State Senate campaign. He accepted the Democratic nomination saying, "For nearly 20 years, Dutchess County and the neighboring counties were represented by those who took orders from two or three men in Chatham and Poughkeepsie... I now accept this nomination with absolute independence and seek only to represent the wishes of the whole district." He pulled off an upset by defeating a Republican incumbent by the largest margin of any Democratic Senate candidate in the state.

The Roosevelts were familiar with Albany, less than two hours from their home in Hyde Park. The family had attended the inauguration of cousin Teddy as Governor in 1899. Franklin's father, James, was a friend of President Grover Cleveland and many who had served in Cleveland's administration back in the 1880s and early 1890s.

As Franklin took the oath of office as a State Senator in 1911, Albany was becoming a modern city of majestic buildings by notable architects. They were being built just a decade after the State Capitol was finally completed in 1899 after thirty years of construction. The Union Station train depot was also completed in this era in 1904. The State Education building behind the State Capitol opened in 1912 with the most Roman columns of any building outside Washington. The spectacular Gothic Flemish Delaware and Hudson railroad building at the bottom of the State Street faced the State Capitol which sat on Capitol hill.

When Franklin Roosevelt arrived to serve in Albany in 1911, he bought a house at 248 State Street, just a block from the State Capitol. He and Eleanor had three children then and brought three servants and two nurses. His mother Sara underwrote much of their expenses which enabled them to live unlike most other legislators who were not financially able to rent more than a room or two in Albany.

Democrats had won control of the New York State Legislature in 1910 with the help of their upstate candidates so Roosevelt would serve in the majority party. Tammany Hall, the political machine in New York City, dominated Democratic politics starting in the 1860s but Roosevelt as an upstate reformer was unwilling to let Tammany control him. Franklin's independent political views were very much in line with his cousin Teddy. Tammany Hall saw young Franklin as cut from the same cloth as his cousin Teddy and thought one Roosevelt was enough.

The new Senator Roosevelt quickly demonstrated his independence and made an impact on a major political issue early in 1911, the appointment of a United States Senator by the State Legislature. Roosevelt's term in Albany was the last before the 17th amendment was ratified by the states in 1913, approving the direct popular election of United States senators. In 1911 though it was still up to the state legislature to elect the state's two senators.

Tammany's New York City Democratic machine leader Charles Murphy had settled on Billy Sheehan of Buffalo to be selected by the

Legislature. Roosevelt joined a group of 21 upstate Democrats who opposed Sheehan and wanted someone more independent of Tammany. They convened regular meetings at Roosevelt's State Street home.

With his famous name, Roosevelt became one of the leaders of the group. When they refused to go along with Sheehan, Murphy didn't have the votes he needed and sent word of a second candidate who was rejected as well. Ironically it was a major fire that devastated part of the State Capitol on the night of March 29, 1911 that helped to resolve the impasse. The fire gutted much of the building including the Assembly and Senate chambers so the legislators had to move across the street to Albany's City Hall to convene in a much smaller space. That inconvenience moved legislators to resolve the issue when Democrats agreed to back Justice James O'Gorman who was proposed by Murphy.

While this nomination was a prominent issue in the first months of the legislative session, it was another fire just four days before the one in the Capitol that would cast a long shadow over the session with calls for progressive reform. On March 25, a fire broke out on the top floors of the Asch Building at Washington Place near Washington Square Park in New York. The fire started by a discarded cigarette butt or lighted match on the top floors in the Triangle Shirtwaist Factory became an historic disaster. With doors locked to prevent workers from taking breaks, 146 persons were killed, some jumping out windows to their deaths. 123 of those killed were women and young children. A witness to the fire was 22 year old Frances Perkins, a young graduate of Mt. Holyoke College who ran the New York office for the national Consumers League. She became a labor activist seeking new laws and regulations to make sure a deadly factory fire never took place again. New York City appointed a Public Safety Committee and Perkins was named to lead it.

The State Legislature also appointed a Factory Investigating Committee led by Assemblyman Al Smith and Senate Majority Leader

Robert Wagner. They toured the state and held hearings into the conditions of hundreds of factories. Over the next two years, the legislature passed 60 bills addressing working and safety conditions which were signed into law by Governor William Sulzer.

Frances Perkins had met young Senator Franklin Roosevelt and was not impressed with him, "I have a vivid picture of him operating on the floor of the Senate, tall and slender, very active and alert, moving around the floor, going in and out of committee rooms, rarely talking with members who more of less avoided him, not particularly charming (that came later), artificially serious of face, rarely smiling, with an unfortunate habit - so natural that he was unaware of it - of throwing his head up. This combined with his pince-nez (glasses) and great height gave him the appearance of looking down his nose at most people." She said he was disliked by many members including Senator Wagner and Assemblyman Al Smith, the two leaders for labor reform that she was championing.

She thought Roosevelt's attitude was the result of "a youthful lack of humility, a streak of self-righteousness, and a deafness to the hopes, fears and aspirations which are the common lot." She was disappointed he was not more active as an advocate for the bills she was pushing. Roosevelt called himself years later, an "awful cuss" in his legislative term.

Meanwhile in Albany, Eleanor would sometimes spend time in the public gallery of the Senate to watch her husband and learn more about the issues being considered. Her attention was not much on politics in those days. She was a mother of three children already. Anna had been born in 1908 followed by James and Elliott. One young son, Franklin Jr. died as a baby. Two more, John and another boy named Franklin, would follow.

The young Senator Roosevelt garnered the attention of a diminutive journalist, Louis Howe, who covered the state capital. He felt that Roosevelt had the skills, personality and character as well as the right name to someday become President of the United States. He left reporting and became Franklin's closest political advisor and operative in Albany and stayed with him throughout his career. He played the key role in charting Franklin's political rise in New York State in the coming years.

When Roosevelt ran for re-election to the Senate in 1912 Tammany Hall wanted to defeat him after he had challenged them on key issues like the Senate appointment. Franklin and Eleanor both came down with typhoid fever from water at their summer home on Campobello Island, leaving Franklin in bed and unable to physically campaign. Louis Howe was eager to take over managing the campaign and he traveled throughout the Senate district. On election day, Roosevelt won again on the strength of Howe's efforts.

In 1912, Franklin threw his support for President to New Jersey Governor Woodrow Wilson and went to meet him in Trenton. He supported Wilson even though Teddy Roosevelt was running on the Bull Moose Party ticket to return to the White House after he split with his successor President William Howard Taft and walked out of the Republican convention. Teddy felt Taft had not been progressive enough and Wilson won easily with Roosevelt second and Taft finishing third in a four way race that included Socialist Eugene Debs. Teddy famously survived an assassination attempt in Milwaukee during the campaign. He was saved by a thick copy of his speech in his coat pocket that took the bullet.

With Wilson's election Franklin Roosevelt had an opportunity in 1913 in the new administration. President Wilson appointed him to take over in March as the Assistant Secretary of the Navy, the same post Teddy Roosevelt had once held in 1897. It was a position that he sought to follow in his cousin's footsteps plus it appealed to Franklin's love of ships and the maritime world. He and Eleanor and the children packed up their Albany home and moved to Washington with the

growing young family. He played a managerial role for the Navy Secretary Josephus Daniels who he had met during the Wilson campaign.

Roosevelt still eyed a career in elective public office. The 17th amendment enabling the direct election of United States Senators took effect
for the 1914 Senate elections. After the approval of the amendment
Franklin decided to run. It was his first statewide contest and despite his
well known name he was easily beaten in the primary by James Gerard,
the US Ambassador to Germany, by a 62%-30% margin. Gerard was
then defeated by Republican James Wadsworth in the general election.

Roosevelt continued in his job with the Navy as world events intervened. The assassination of Austrian Archduke Ferdinand plunged
Europe into the Great War, later known as World War I. Though the
United States remained out of the war in its early years, Roosevelt's
navy role was an important one. He visited naval installations in the
United States and worked on preparedness with the belief that the nation would eventually be drawn into it.

Each summer he and Eleanor would escape the summer heat and
humidity of Washington. They would spend time at homes owned by
his mother Sara at Campobello Island off the coast of Maine. Franklin
was working and would show up on a navy vessel at Campobello.

In 1916, an epidemic of polio or I.P. infantile paralysis swept
the country. There were 27,000 cases across the country with 6,000
deaths. The outbreak was severe in New York City where 2000 died.
People were in a panic and fled upstate to the Catskills. Movie theaters
were closed, public meetings were canceled and public life came to a
standstill. As parents Franklin and Eleanor were concerned about getting the children home safely. Franklin sent a letter to Eleanor, "Swat
every fly in the house at Campobello and do not think about bringing
the children back by train or by automobile, since some New England
villages were blocking out of town cars with children in them." They
finally were able to use the USS Dolphin to evacuate them from the

island and head home. Back at Hyde Park the children were quarantined until the epidemic subsided.

As the 1916 Presidential election began, Teddy Roosevelt decided not to accept the nomination of the Progressive Party to run again. President Wilson was re-elected narrowly defeating Republican Charles Evans Hughes. Franklin remained working for Wilson at the Navy Department. By 1917, the United States was drawn into the war after the sinking of the Lusitania with hundreds of Americans on board. Teddy Roosevelt urged Franklin to join the armed forces but President Wilson wanted him to remain in his administration. Eleanor volunteered as a Red Cross nurse to help wounded soldiers in Washington and she raised money to provide a center for therapy. Her uncle Teddy sent her $5000 to support the effort.

As Assistant Secretary of the Navy, Franklin Roosevelt had toured Europe to inspect United States forces and the battlefields in the fall of 1918 as the war was drawing to a close. While in England as a guest of King George V at a dinner he met Winston Churchill, the Minister of Munitions. (Years later FDR reminded Churchill of their first meeting and Churchill couldn't remember it).

An epidemic of a flu that originated in Spain besieged the world and the United States in 1918-1920. 675,000 Americans died with nearly five million sick. FDR returned home from Europe on a ship, the USS Leviathan, where the virus was rampant and he became one of hundreds on the vessel who got the flu and double pneumonia. He was taken on a stretcher from the ambulance to his house on East 65th Street in Manhattan.

Roosevelt's name again surfaced for statewide office in 1918 when some suggested him as a candidate for Governor. He would have to leave his important Navy job during World War I and it was assumed that Republicans would say in the campaign that Roosevelt put ambition above his service to the government in wartime.

Al Smith, then the Assembly Speaker, got the nomination for Governor and won the general election. Roosevelt certainly had his sights set on a future run for office in New York when the right opportunity presented itself. However, his political future had nearly been derailed at that time after Eleanor discovered love letters while Franklin was sick and she unpacked his suitcase. The letters confirmed the affair she suspected he was having with Lucy Mercer, the secretary Eleanor had hired. The discovery created a crisis in their marriage and forever changed it. Eleanor had offered Franklin the opportunity to get out of the marriage with a divorce. However divorce in those years would have been fatal for Roosevelt's political future as Louis Howe told him and he agreed to end his relationship and rebuild his marriage with Eleanor. Their marriage was no longer a love affair but a partnership in both family and public interests. Eleanor supported Franklin's political aspirations despite the roles she would have to play which she did so loyally.

In 1919, the country was exhausted by the war, the Spanish flu pandemic, and the anti-Communist Palmer raids. In July and August 1919 racial riots swept across Chicago and over twenty other cities as African Americans migrated north and veterans returned home to discrimination. The postwar years of 1919 and 1920 were also marked by dramatic political changes including the passage of two more Constitutional amendments. The 18th amendment, the Volstead Act, established Prohibition in January 1919 and the 19th amendment was passed which approved women's suffrage nationwide on August 19, 1920.

Teddy Roosevelt was planning on running for President again on the Republican ticket in 1920 thinking it was an ideal chance for a Republican to win after the war and with the country hungry for change. However, Teddy died suddenly in his sleep on January 6, 1919. It was a terrible blow for the family and the legendary Teddy's death created political opportunities for other family members with political aspirations.

His son, Ted Jr. was the focus of a great deal of attention in the fall of 1919 as he launched his own political career, winning an Assembly seat on Long Island. He was already thinking of a future that might lead to the Governor's mansion and beyond.

In 1920 the Wilson Administration was winding down with a sick president whose efforts were failing to gain Congressional passage of United States membership in the League of Nations in the aftermath of the end of World War I. The country was looking for normalcy. Franklin Roosevelt was still serving as the Assistant Secretary of the Navy in the federal government and had been thinking of running for Governor or Senator from New York State. However, he had also tried to convince the respected Herbert Hoover, known as the "Great Humanitarian" for leading war relief efforts, to run for President as a Democrat and perhaps Franklin would be his running mate.

Franklin and Eleanor met with Hoover in March 1920. Colonel Edward House, a top aide to President Woodrow Wilson, said: "It's a wonderful idea. A Hoover-Roosevelt ticket is probably the only chance the Democrats have in November." Hoover later announced though that he would seek the Republican nomination. He lost as the GOP chose instead Senator Warren G. Harding of Ohio as its nominee with Governor Calvin Coolidge of Massachusetts as his running mate.

The eventual Democratic nominee was another Ohioan, Governor James Cox, and he chose Roosevelt as his running mate despite the fact he had never won a statewide race. Over 8000 people showed up at the Roosevelt's Springwood home in Hyde Park when Roosevelt was notified of his nomination for Vice President and then heard his acceptance speech. He spoke to the crowd, saying, "We oppose money in politics, we oppose the private control of national finances, we oppose the treatment of human beings as commodities, we oppose the saloon-bossed city, we oppose starvation wages, we oppose rule by groups or cliques." He was also a strong supporter of Woodrow Wilson and his advocacy to establish the League of Nations to resolve international disputes.

Two days later, Franklin undertook a vigorous barnstorming train campaign as he crisscrossed the country and later spoke in New York State which was a key swing state in the election. He made 800 speeches and traveled to 40 states.

Louis Howe put together a campaign team that included some who would be with FDR throughout his political career including Marguerite LeHand, a personal assistant who became one of his closest personal confidants and in later years stood in for Eleanor at some meetings. She was born in Potsdam, New York and grew up in Somerville, Massachusetts. A Southerner, Steve Early, was his advance man who later became his press secretary Meanwhile, his cousin, Republican Teddy Roosevelt Jr. followed him around and created a political rift in the family as he tried to discredit Franklin saying, "He is a maverick - he does not have the brand of our family."

1920 was not a good year for the Democrats. With the country looking for change, the Cox-Roosevelt ticket was easily defeated by seven million votes by the Republican Harding-Coolidge ticket. Harding beat Cox by two to one in New York State and Governor Al Smith was defeated for re-election.

# CHAPTER 2

## Polio and the Turning Point

AFTER THE DEFEAT of the Cox-Roosevelt ticket, Roosevelt resigned from the Navy Department and he joined a law firm with two friends, Langdon Marvin and Grenville Emmett. He also took a job as Vice President of the Fidelity and Deposit Company in their New York office. He accepted many requests to help numerous charitable organizations including the Boy Scouts, the Near East Committee, the Lighthouse for the Blind, the Navy Club and others. He was also an overseer for Harvard University and was a leader in establishing the Woodrow Wilson Foundation.

Franklin Roosevelt had survived the Spanish flu in 1918 but soon his political ascension in 1920 would be bookended by a catastrophic health crisis that would forever change his life. In the summer of 1921, the family again spent time at their home on Campobello Island. Franklin enjoyed days on the water with his children and friends including Louis Howe. One day after swimming and boating, he became very weak and unable to move some parts of his body. A doctor was summoned from the area who thought it was a blood clot. Franklin had a 102 degree fever and his condition worsened. His uncle Warren Delano made a contact with Dr. Robert Lovett in Boston who came to the island and determined he had contracted polio which was killing thousands every year. Roosevelt couldn't believe it. To him polio was a "babies disease."

Within days he was paralyzed below his armpits and his life was unalterably changed. He couldn't urinate for weeks. Louis Howe made sure that the public did not see the condition he was in or know how sick he really was. Roosevelt had to be transported by boat and train and airlifted back to New York on September 14. He was taken to Presbyterian Hospital where he remained until being released to his East 65th Street home on October 28.

The *New York Times* reported that he had polio and the prognosis was good. This was based on a deliberately more optimistic statement written by Louis Howe that said he was paralyzed below the knees rather than below his chest except for some use of his arms and hands. His personal physician and Groton classmate, Dr. George Draper, who was an expert in polio was quoted in the statement saying, "He will not be crippled." Privately, he doubted then if he would ever sit up again.

Roosevelt's political future was more than put on hold. His mother, Sara, clashed with Franklin and Eleanor because she wanted him to return to Hyde Park to live and rehabilitate. Franklin and Eleanor felt he needed to remain in New York to be close to his work and associates.

Franklin and others were unsure if he would ever have the stamina and strength to run and hold office. He spent months at home recuperating. He was determined to recover though and to remain connected with community and public affairs. He agreed to sit on a Vassar College endowment committee and he accepted an appointment to the Executive Committee of the New York State Democratic Committee. He continued to be associated with his law firm. He and Louis Howe also got involved in a lot of speculative investment schemes, some of which included slot machines, lobster traps and zeppelins.

In 1922, his name was mentioned as a possible candidate for Governor but he was in no condition to run. William Randolph Hearst was running for the Democratic nomination. Roosevelt disliked him and he and Eleanor actively encouraged and supported Al Smith who was trying to regain the Governor's seat he lost in 1920. Roosevelt's support boosted Smith who won the primary and the general election to return to Albany as Governor in 1923.

Of course, the most important person in the life and political career of Franklin Roosevelt was his wife, Eleanor. It was during those years when Franklin was in rehabilitation that she became his political stand-in under the guidance of Louis Howe. He coached her on how to speak and present herself. She had never cared for Howe and his involvement with Franklin but she had grown in respect for him as a person during the 1920 Vice Presidential campaign when she spent a lot of time with him on the campaign trail. Though she was interested and active in civic causes, she had never seen herself as pursuing her own public career but supporting her husband.

She became an avid feminist and activist just as women had gained the right to vote and were becoming more influential in public life. She worked with Esther Lape and her partner Elizabeth Read who were involved in many activist organizations including the League of Women Voters which grew out of the suffragette movement.

Eleanor also became involved in the Consumers League and in 1924, she became the Chairwoman of the new women's division of the New York State Democratic party. In that role, she immediately challenged the Tammany leadership and insisted that women would not be taken for granted and have no real power in the party. Tammany Hall leader Charles Murphy planned to select the women who would attend the 1924 national convention in New York City. Eleanor was determined that women should select their own delegates to the convention. At Albany's Ten Eyck Hotel she spoke to a woman's meeting and said, "To many women, and I am one of them, it is extraordinarily difficult to care about anything enough to cause disagreement or unpleasant feelings, but I have come to the conclusion that this be done for a time until we can prove our strength and demand respect for our wishes." She had a showdown with Murphy and went around him to Governor Al Smith who overruled Murphy.

## Re-emergence in Public Life

In 1923, President Warren G. Harding had died unexpectedly and Vice President Calvin Coolidge had become President. Despite the Teapot Dome scandal that had marred Harding's administration, the economy was riding so high after the war that the decade would become known as the Roaring Twenties. Automobiles and radios were being mass produced and the new modern prosperous era was changing the American way of life in previous decades. Americans could travel farther and be more connected to the nation and the world as the era of the horse and buggy came to an end.

In 1924, Governor Al Smith, a Catholic, decided to run for the Democratic presidential nomination. Franklin Roosevelt had been working with Dr. William McDonald, a neurologist in Marion, Massachusetts to try to strengthen his muscles so that he would not have to use braces to walk. Louis Howe had remained as Roosevelt's top political assistant and he promoted Roosevelt for roles in the Democratic Party. It was at the 1924 Democratic convention that he made his political return when he was asked by Al Smith to be his convention manager and to place his name in nomination for President.

Roosevelt and Smith had become political allies but they had come from very different personal backgrounds. Smith was a descendant of Irish immigrants and he was champion of the working class. Roosevelt came from a wealthy family history with relatives going back to the American revolution. It was in 1920 though that Smith saw Franklin

Roosevelt as an asset for him. With his wealth and political pedigree Roosevelt could give Smith an aura of political acceptability. Roosevelt had given the seconding speech for Smith's nomination for President at the 1920 Democratic convention. In 1924, Howe and Roosevelt helped Smith to gain delegates in the nomination battle with William McAdoo of California, the son in law of Woodrow Wilson. Roosevelt even wrote a letter asking Babe Ruth to endorse Smith which he did.

As he entered the convention hall to nominate Smith, the nation and especially the Democrats were keenly aware of the long recuperation of the man who had four years earlier been their Vice Presidential nominee. His son Elliott recalled, "Father had set his heart on walking alone onto the rostrum. On Jimmy's arm, he made his way up the aisle to the rear of the platform. He asked a delegate to go shake the podium so he could know if he would bear his weight. He let go of my brother's arm, grasped his second crutch from Jimmy and swung himself forward until he could grip the edges of the stand. The crowd roared its approval. He dared not let go of a hand to acknowledge the cheers; a broad smile had to serve the purpose."

The early summer heat at the Madison Square Garden convention hall left Roosevelt heavily perspiring. Frances Perkins who was sitting close to the podium saw that his body was tensed and shaking. Any concerns about his political ability arising from his physical condition evaporated when he gave an exuberant speech saying Smith was crusading for the working person and he called him "the happy warrior," a label which stayed with Smith.

The 1924 convention famously became deadlocked between Smith and McAdoo and took 103 ballots over two weeks. The Ku Klux Klan was riding high in the mid 1920s and they opposed the anti-Prohibition, big city, Irish Catholic Smith. He had a New York accent and said "raddio" for radio and was viewed in the South and other parts of the country like a Vaudeville character. Many felt that if the smiling, charming Roosevelt had been in better health he could have walked away with the nomination as the compromise candidate though 1924 was not a good year for any Democrat to try to unseat President Coolidge.

Finally, the convention settled on John W. Davis of West Virginia, a former Solicitor General and Ambassador to Great Britain under Woodrow Wilson as its compromise presidential nominee. Coolidge rode the prosperity of the 1920s to a wide victory with Davis only winning the traditionally Democratic Solid South from Virginia to Texas. Progressive candidate Robert Lafollette won 16.6% of the vote and won his home state of Wisconsin.

The defeated Smith decided to run that fall for re-election as Governor. His Republican opponent was Theodore Roosevelt Jr. At the time, he was the third Roosevelt to serve as Assistant Secretary of the Navy when Harding appointed him to the post. Teddy Jr. viewed himself as his father's rightful political heir, rather than Franklin. He also hoped to follow his father's footsteps from the Navy job to Governor and then to the White House.

Louis Howe devised a campaign strategy for Smith which included Eleanor touring the state with a Teapot to reflect the Republican scandal and to trail her first cousin Teddy Jr. as he campaigned. She traveled around the state with her women colleagues, Marion Dickerman and Nancy Cook, and created a family uproar with her criticisms and Teddy Jr. never forgave her.

Smith was elected again to a third term, beating Teddy Jr. by 108,000 votes, or about 3%, 50% to 47%.

Smith ran again for a fourth, two-year term in 1926 and he asked Franklin to nominate him at the state Democratic convention in Syracuse. Smith won again by a wide margin over Republican Ogden Mills. Edwin Corning of Albany was elected as his Lt. Governor. There was interest among some leading Democrats to have Roosevelt run for the US Senate in 1926 but he said he needed more time to rehabilitate himself and to walk better.

Smith was a trailblazing, progressive Governor during his four terms. He led the modernization of state government through a re-organization which produced greater efficiency in state agencies and also gave the Governor greater control over the budget process. That was a significant change because the Governor won the power to propose an overall budget rather than each agency submitting its own to the Legislature, a chaotic and inefficient process.

## Therapy in Warm Springs, Georgia

Roosevelt began to spend winters in Florida and sailed on his house-boat, the Larooco, in 1924. He was often with Missy LeHand, his secretary and companion, and they spent days on the water.

In 1924 he heard about the Meriwether resort in Warm Springs, Georgia that had shown some benefits from its mineral springs for those suffering from polio. It was an old resort that had been popular before the Civil War but had fallen into disrepair. George Peabody, a wealthy businessman and philanthropist originally from Georgia who was active in Democratic politics purchased the resort and invited Franklin to visit it and then buy it. Peabody had chaired the state commission to preserve the mineral waters spa in Saratoga Springs, New York following the death of his business partner, Spencer Trask of Saratoga.

Roosevelt paid a visit in October 1924 and found that the extensive water therapy in Warm Springs improved his condition. The water springing from a side of a mountain was 88 degrees. He worked with Dr. LeRoy Hubbard, an orthopedic surgeon from the New York State Board of Health with experience with polio patients. This water therapy was more promising than his muscle exercises with Dr. McDonald as he was able to walk in the warm water without crutches and braces.

Roosevelt liked the area which was in the rural south and he began to spend extended periods of time there with Missy LeHand. Eleanor would join him sometimes and she had family connections. Her grandmother, Teddy Roosevelt's mother, had lived in Georgia. However, Eleanor was not as comfortable with the segregationist society there.

Franklin traveled around the area in Georgia and became such a well known public speaker that some Georgians were discussing him as a candidate for Governor since he had a residence in the state. He deflected any political speculation by saying he needed to continue his therapy so that he could be stronger and able to do more.

Roosevelt decided he wanted to revive the resort as a health spa. He invested a substantial part of his assets to buy the old resort and 1700 acres of farmland and he established the Warm Springs Foundation. He purchased it on April 29, 1926 and it began to attract people who had heard of his improvement from its waters and more people came to stay. Many were poor and Roosevelt helped to provide housing and support for them. Roosevelt enjoyed playing in the water with other patients, especially the children who called him "Dr. Roosevelt." Serving people with disabilities, especially young children became a cause of his life. He would spend most of the year there except for summers and the Christmas holiday when he was back in Hyde Park.

Meanwhile, Eleanor had gone into business too, joining with her friends Nancy Cook and Marion Dickerman to start Val Kill Industries to make reproductions of quality furniture. Franklin had agreed to build Val Kill as a cottage home for Eleanor and her friends and it was from there that they began the furniture production. Eleanor was offered the opportunity to become a teacher at the Todhunter School for girls in Manhattan and she, Dickerman and Cook purchased it.

Eleanor also continued her political activities with the women's division of the state Democratic party. She and Franklin were now pursuing separate interests though she remained committed to supporting him when he and Louis Howe felt he was ready to run for office again.

# CHAPTER 3

## *The 1928 Election*

AL SMITH HAD NOT given up his presidential dream and in 1928 he made another White House bid. For the third time Franklin Roosevelt was at the national convention in Houston to give a nominating address and told the delegates, "I am rather pleased with the fact that I, in company with you, formed the Alfred E. Smith habit a long time ago." Humorist Will Rogers was heard to remark after the convention, "That fellow Franklin Roosevelt, if you woke him up in the middle of his nap, he would start in nominating Alfred J. Smith."

Smith finally won the Democratic presidential nomination, the first Catholic in American history. He would be vacating the Executive Mansion in Albany and he sought someone to succeed him as the Democratic nominee for Governor who could help him win the state in the Presidential race. New York was important in the Electoral College. Not only did it have the most electoral votes but it was considered a swing state at that time.

Many felt the nominee should be an upstate Protestant, not another Catholic or a Jewish candidate like Herbert Lehman, a partner in Lehman Brothers, his family's investment banking firm. Smith's Lt. Governor, Edwin Corning of Albany, was considered a possibility to run but an illness sidelined him. John Boyd Thacher II, the Albany Mayor, was also a possibility as was Congressman Peter Ten Eyck of Albany. Owen D. Young, the prominent business leader was considered as well as Robert Wagner. It was Roosevelt though who Smith decided would be the best candidate to help him in New York and who might help him nationally too with his well known name.

A re-entry into politics in 1928 was not in Roosevelt's plans. He wanted to spend more time in Warm Springs continuing his recuperation that was making him physically stronger. Louis Howe and Eleanor also did not want him to run. Howe felt the timing was not right. He believed that a Republican would likely win the White House again as the economy continued to be strong. Howe also felt that losing would destroy Franklin's future chances and that his disability would be cited as a reason for his defeat since many privately wondered if he was physically up for the job.

Howe felt that Herbert Hoover, the Republican nominee, would win two terms and that it would not be until 1936 before a better opportunity would arise for Roosevelt to run for President. He felt Roosevelt had time to run for Governor in the early 1930s to position himself for a future White House run.

Eleanor Roosevelt explained, "Louis Howe was not happy about Franklin's candidacy. He always thought in terms of the future, and he had planned that Franklin should be a candidate four or eight years thence. Louis feared that if Governor Smith lost nationally, it might not be possible for Franklin to carry the state for the governorship, which might spoil any chance he had for future political office." Eleanor also did not welcome the idea of having to subordinate her civic and political activities if she became the state's first lady.

In 1928 she became a member of the advisory committee for women's activities of the Democratic national committee and worked on Al Smith's presidential campaign. So, as the state Democratic convention opened in Rochester Eleanor was there while Franklin was in Warm Springs actively resisting any effort to get him to consider running. He had indicated to the press weeks before that he did not want to be considered as a candidate for Governor.

Just a week earlier, for the first time, he had walked a few steps without aid and he wanted to continue toward that goal. Missy LeHand told him, "Don't you dare," when he was being pressured to run.

Smith had been trying unsuccessfully to reach Franklin to recruit him to run for Governor. Finally, Smith asked Eleanor to intervene before she left the convention. He asked her to get Franklin on the phone so he could make another attempt to change his mind. Roosevelt was purposely away from his residence in Warm Springs and the phone so he wouldn't have to speak to Smith. Eleanor did get him on the phone though and she then passed it on to Smith as she left for her train trip home.

Smith and his close aides also thought that Roosevelt would not have the strength to run a vigorous campaign or even serve as Governor and that they would continue to run the state in key posts with Roosevelt. So Smith told Roosevelt that he would only have to give a few speeches and Lehman, the candidate for Lt. Governor, would do most of the campaigning.

Roosevelt was also concerned about the financial viability of his Warm Springs resort. He may have become more willing to consider the race when John Raskob, one of the wealthy leaders of the State Democratic committee and an ally of Al Smith, said he would make a substantial contribution to the foundation. Smith was adamant, telling Roosevelt the convention would be at a stalemate and the party's chances at the state and national level depended on his decision. Smith finally asked Roosevelt if he would decline the nomination if the delegates selected him. Not hearing a firm no Smith got the delegates to nominate Roosevelt.

On October 16, 1928, Roosevelt's name was placed in nomination by New York City Mayor Jimmy Walker. In the end, Roosevelt felt an obligation to serve. Roosevelt addressed the state party and said, "I accept the nomination for Governor because I am a disciple in a great cause. I have been enlisted as a private in the ranks for many years and I cannot fail to heed a call for more active service in a time when so much is at stake."

Eleanor wrote in her autobiography, "I did not know until the following morning when I bought a newspaper that my husband had been persuaded finally to accept the nomination."

The Democratic platform included an eight hour work day and forty eight hour work week for women and children in industry, consideration of old age pensions, and an advisory minimum wage board. The platform also supported direct primaries for all state offices, a limit on campaign expenditures, perpetual state ownership of state water power resources, support for farms, a four year term for Governor, a biennial session of the state legislature and four year terms for state senators and two year terms for Assemblymembers who then faced election every year. The platform also would leave alcohol laws to the states rather than continue Prohibition. It was a tumultuous time and the winner would enter office during the Prohibition era when the capital city of Albany was described as "dripping wet" and facing enforcement raids against speakeasies.

The Republicans nominated state Attorney General Albert Ottinger and his line of attack against Roosevelt was focused on Tammany Hall corruption. Ottinger was an economic conservative and wanted to abolish the income tax. He tried to straddle the Prohibition issue to appeal to those who opposed it.

The Republicans also publicly raised Roosevelt's health and said that his nomination was unfair to him and the people of the state because of his condition. They didn't understand his determination and stamina though.

He had written out a retort to them, "I am deeply touched by the tender solicitude displayed by my Republican adversaries first as to my anguish of mind and now as to the feebleness of my body. I trust I have convinced them that the martyr's crown was not being pressed upon my head and I would like at this early date in order to clear the way for discussion of good government and vital state issues to reassure them as to my physical condition. Let me soothe their fears by explaining that the impossibility of engaging in exhaustive physical exercise has enabled me to take far better care of my health than most men as actively engaged in business as I have been for the last four years."

By 1928, Roosevelt was able to walk by using just a cane while holding an arm of his son or an aide. Rather than be a physically limited candidate, Roosevelt undertook a vigorous campaign and traveled across the entire state, driving to the small towns and counties of upstate New York. He made thirty three major addresses and many informal ones. He began in the Southern Tier speaking in Binghamton where he was greeted by hundreds at the railroad station and then spoke before 2500 at the high school auditorium.

In his remarks there supporting Smith, Roosevelt spoke out strongly against religious bigotry aimed at Smith's Catholicism by forces including the Ku Klux Klan which was very active in the Binghamton area. He also said he did not want a single vote because of his opponent Ottinger's Jewish faith. He went much further and said the "attacks on Smith's religion should be punished by deportation, this un-American, this vile thing that is hanging over our heads." His words were so strong and controversial that some of his aides sent word that this issue was not something that would help politically and that he was running for Governor not President.

Al Smith's daughter, Catherine, had been wed at the Cathedral of the Immaculate Conception in Albany in June of that year and a special blessing was sent by Pope Pius XI through New York's Cardinal

Hayes who presided over the ceremony. Some were worried that news reels would be shown in the Protestant South with the Cardinal and his court at the Catholic wedding ceremony.

Roosevelt went on to campaign in Deposit, Port Jervis, Hancock, Owego, Elmira, Corning, Hornell, Wellsville, Olean, Salamanca, Jamestown. Then, he spoke in Batavia, Seneca Falls, Dunkirk, Canandaigua, Oswego, Watertown, Boonville, Rome, Utica, Herkimer, Schenectady, Troy, and Albany.

Roosevelt's campaign speeches were often more about supporting Al Smith's presidential bid than about his own plans for Governor. He did have some key issues from the party platform he stressed including public ownership of water power resources at Niagara Falls and the St. Lawrence River and passing a pension program for older persons

In Rochester on October 21, two weeks after he was nominated there, he spoke about the plight of the elderly who had to live in poorhouses as they aged, couldn't find work and didn't have any savings or pensions. He talked about his own feelings saying, "I think one of the most oppressing things· that I have to do on occasion in this state is to visit the County Poorhouse. Somehow it just tears my heart to see those old men and women there, more than almost anything that I know. We need a drastic revision of the poor laws, and I propose to recommend it." He added, "I suppose that those of us, who, this coming winter, ask for an immediate study of the question of old-age pensions, will be written down as Bolsheviks."

His sons and others held his arms as he stood to make speeches. He told the media, "No movies of me getting out of the machine, boys" and they obliged. So the public usually just saw him standing upright or perhaps moving with canes or crutches. His son, Elliott, wrote about one campaign appearance, "he had to be carried up a fire escape into one meeting hall and (son) Jimmy, who came back from another trip to Europe with Granny to help in the campaign came close to tears again when he saw Father being lifted over obstacles, 'like a sack of potatoes'." The struggle he had was known only to a few.

Campaigning in Watertown, Roosevelt complimented the community for its municipally owned power system that provided electricity for city street lights and the excess power was sold and generated income for the city. He was a strong supporter of workers and got the endorsement of the Central Trade and Labor Council of New York City which represented 60,000 workers.

Roosevelt closed his campaign tour in New York City, speaking at the end of October in Flushing, Bronx, Manhattan, Brooklyn and also Yonkers.

The final rally had 20,000 people on Main Street in Poughkeepsie on November 5 and then 200 friends gathered in front of his Springwood home in Hyde Park on the night of the election.

With the economy on a bull run in the Roaring 1920s, Republican nominee Herbert Hoover was able to capitalize on it while Smith was battered by the anti-Catholic bigotry and was easily defeated, 58%-41%. Commentators said he was defeated by the 3 Ps: Prohibition, Prejudice and Prosperity. He even lost New York State by over 103,000 votes and only won in New York City, Albany County and three other upstate counties.

Franklin Roosevelt went to bed on election night feeling that he too would be submerged in the Republican national tide just as Eleanor and Louis Howe feared. However, when he woke the next morning, he learned that he had defeated Albert Ottinger by just 25,564 votes out of 4.23 million, 49% to 48%, to become the Governor-elect of New York. He ran behind Smith's total in New York City by 32,000 votes but he managed to get 70,000 more votes than Smith upstate. Democratic State Party Chair James Farley rebuilt the organization in upstate and rural areas that had not been effectively organized for Democrats since Grover Cleveland ran for Governor in 1882. The campaign spent $438,000.

Ottinger refused to concede for twelve days when he finally offered cordial cooperation. Eighteen years after he first was elected a State Senator from the Hudson Valley, Franklin Roosevelt was headed back to Albany to lead the Empire State and live in the Executive Mansion.

Despite his vigorous campaign for the governor's office, the status of Roosevelt's health continued to be a prime topic of public and private discussion before he was inaugurated. Al Smith reportedly said Roosevelt wouldn't last a year as Governor. Rumors circulated that he might resign before taking office or that his physical condition might also inflict his mind at some point.

Roosevelt would no longer have the freedom to spend as much time in Warm Springs. On December 16, 1928 though he announced from Hyde Park that he had a visit with Stuart Greene, the State Superintendent of Public Works. Mr. Greene informed him that Roosevelt's wish and plan for a heated pool to be constructed behind the Governor's mansion in Albany had been approved. Two of three greenhouses would be demolished and a third would be converted to a pool that would be heated to approximate conditions in Warm Springs. The Executive Mansion also had ramps installed and was made accessible for his wheelchair.

A day before the inauguration, the *New York Times* reported that Roosevelt's doctor in Warm Springs stated that his patient would be able to do the job but he needed to maintain his strict health and exercise regimen of getting to bed by 10:30 and up by 9:30 with a nap in the middle of the day.

# CHAPTER 4

## *Governor Franklin D. Roosevelt*

1000 PEOPLE WERE STANDING along the driveway to the Executive Mansion on Eagle Street to welcome Franklin and Eleanor Roosevelt as they arrived in Albany on New Year's Eve, December 31, 1928, for his inauguration the next day. Most though were there to say goodbye to Governor Al Smith who had spent eight years in Albany as Governor during his four two-year terms, beginning in 1919. As the Roosevelt car pulled under the portico at the mansion, Governor and Mrs. Smith were waiting for them. Smith later departed the mansion but returned to host a dinner in the evening. After dinner, Roosevelt was officially sworn in as Governor on the family's Dutch Bible from the 1600s by Judge Irving Lehman, the brother of the new Lt. Governor.

On January 1, 1929 Secretary of State Robert Moses publicly administered the oath of office again to Franklin Delano Roosevelt who at age 46 became the 48th Governor of New York before a large crowd packed inside the Assembly Chamber in the State Capitol. Outside, a 17 cannon salute followed. Hundreds of people from all over the state and some out of state visitors were on hand along with Eleanor and their children and Franklin's mother, Sara Delano Roosevelt. A special ramp had to be constructed for Roosevelt to make his way to the podium.

Before the oath was administered, tradition was broken when Governor Smith was introduced and delivered a farewell address. He noted how state government had grown and that a new 34-story office tower, was being completed facing the State Capitol. That building was later named for him. He talked about the good condition of the state's finances. He recalled how he had first come to the city as a member of the Assembly twenty years earlier in 1909 and said he would miss the many friends he had made in Albany.

Smith congratulated Roosevelt's family and his mother Sara seated there and told the Roosevelt children he was leaving many animals in the zoo at the mansion. "He had a petting zoo in the backyard that had several animals at one point including seven dogs, one elk, three bears, four raccoons, one possum, four monkeys, one goat, one donkey, two ponies, rabbits, barn owls, and pheasants, " the *New York Times* reported.

Smith was born and lived his entire life in New York City except during his time as Governor in Albany. Roosevelt prided himself on his agricultural background and he could more easily relate to upstaters. He loved the land where he was born and lived and he wanted to champion the interests of farmers and conservation. Even their voices gave away their differences. Roosevelt had a patrician formality in his voice which contrasted with Smith's working class manner of speaking.

Franklin Roosevelt entered office in the long shadow of Smith's four terms as Governor. Roosevelt would be inheriting Smith's reforms of state government that gave the Governor more executive powers. In his inaugural address Roosevelt honored Smith for his service and accomplishments, saying, "I am certain that no Governor in the long history of the State has accomplished more than he in definite improvement of the structure of our state government, in the wise, efficient and honorable administration of its affairs and finally in his possession of that vibrant understanding heart attuned to the needs and hopes of the men, the women and the children who form the sovereignty known as the People of the State New York."

Roosevelt then presented his own view of the importance and value of government. He argued against the prevailing American individualism, "For it is literally true that the self supporting man or woman has become as extinct as the man of the Stone Age...I am proud that we of this state have grown to realize this dependence, and what is more important, have also come to know that we, as individuals, in our turn must give our time and intelligence to help those who have helped us."

He extolled the empire state for its progressivism. "It is a proud thing to be a citizen of the State of New York, not because of our great population and our natural resources, nor on account of our industries, our trade, or our agricultural development but because the citizens of the state more than any other state in the union have come to realize the interdependence on each other which modern civilization has created."

He laid out an expansive vision of what society and government should be for all the people, "To insure more of life's pleasure for the farmer; to guard toilers in the factories and to insure them a fair wage and protection from the dangers of the trade; to compensate them by adequate insurance for injuries received while working for us, to open the doors of knowledge to their children more widely, to aid those who are crippled and ill, to pursue with strict justice all evil persons who prey upon their fellow-men and, by intelligent and helpful sympathy to lead wrongdoers into right paths. All of these great aims of life are more fully realized here than in any other State of the Union."

He concluded by speaking for common purpose and against partisan politics, saying, "There is a period in our history known in all our school books as the 'Era of Good Feeling.' It is my hope that we stand on the threshold of another such era in this State."

He hoped to put an end to the partisan squabbling but he also showed his political instincts by suggesting that the voters would have a say again in two years if the public will was not followed. He spoke of three pressing issues including public water power, judicial reform and farm aid.

He wanted to make life better for farmers. Early in his administration he had appointed an Agricultural Advisory Commission which had studied the impact of taxes and state policies on farming. Since the cost of many services was financed by property taxes, the Commission made recommendations for the state to assume more local costs which would then lower taxes on land owned by farmers.

Public power was an issue that he felt very strongly about and an important topic of public interest. He made it clear that the great natural resource of water and the electrical power it could generate should not be in private hands but should go to the benefit of the people. "The title to this power must vest forever in the people of this State. No commission, no, not the Legislature itself has any right to give, for any consideration whatever, a single potential kilowatt in virtual perpetuity to any person or corporation whatsoever."

The next day, January 2, Roosevelt gave his address to the Legislature, or the State of the State address as it would later be commonly known. Despite his own victory, Roosevelt was facing a Legislature with both houses controlled by the Republicans who were dominant in the 1920s. There were 27 Republicans and 24 Democrats in the 51 seat State Senate which was elected every two years. Republicans also controlled the 150 seat Assembly elected every year. The state budget enacted in 1929 was $265 million and there would be almost 12.6 million residents of New York State in the 1930 Census the next year, up from 10.4 million or 21% from the 1920 Census.

One of the Republicans in the Assembly was suffragette, Rhoda Fox Graves of Gouverneur in St. Lawrence County, the only woman in the Legislature. She was the first woman in both the Assembly and later the Senate and the first woman to chair a Senate Committee.

Roosevelt opened his address to the legislators by again calling on them to put partisanship aside and serve the best interests of the people. He discussed the usual laundry list of state issues and operations including agriculture, labor, parks, budget issues, public works, judicial reform, election law reform, local government relations,  health care, waterpower and energy. He also added some unique issues at that time that were subtitled in his written remarks.  One was "Cripples," the term commonly used  then for persons with physical disabilities. Of course, this was a personal issue to Roosevelt as a polio survivor. Many disabled persons were housed in state facilities which he considered inadequate and he called for major changes.  Later, he discussed making the mineral waters at Saratoga Springs a destination for those with physical ailments.

The new governor also devoted a section of his speech to enacting a state Constitutional amendment that would increase the term of office for the Governor to four years, a change that had been discussed for years. He challenged the legislators to trust the decision to the people if they would not take action in the Legislature, "If you are unwilling to pass a new constitutional amendment,  which is my recommendation, providing for the election in off years,  I ask you in fairness to submit this simple question to the voters by referendum for an expression of their opinion at the next November election."

## Life at the Executive Mansion

The Executive Mansion on Eagle Street in Albany became the focus of a whirlwind of business and social activity.  The Roosevelts and their five children, several of whom were teenagers, all lived in the mansion. There were nine bedrooms and some were often occupied by aides or friends.  Eleanor hosted tea in the afternoons for guests.  Roosevelt's secretary, Missy LeHand, had a room in the mansion that connected to his master suite. She had become one of his closest aides in Albany and in later years when FDR was in the the White House. She would often serve as hostess at events while Eleanor was away.

Frances Perkins recalled, "There were nieces, nephews, cousins, school friends of the Roosevelt boys. Roosevelt moved in this family commotion with joyous relish. They entertained a great deal, inviting people to dinner from all over the state. If a person came from a distance, there was often an invitation to spend the night at the Executive Mansion. Night after night every bed was full and visiting friends of long acquaintance were asked to double up."

She described what it was like to be a visitor to the mansion, "Visiting at the Executive Mansion which I often did in Albany, was like staying at an agreeable home furnished in a slightly Victorian manner. The place did not confine the Roosevelts to a formal pattern; they took it in stride, they moved the furniture around, fixed up a cozy little sitting room upstairs, brought a few things from Hyde Park and made it look more like home than like the property of the State of New York. Coats, books, papers were left around all over the Mansion, giving it that pleasantly occupied look."

There were fifteen state paid servants and every room had a push button to call them. A cook and chauffeur were not included so the Roosevelts paid for those positions. Eleanor Roosevelt wrote about the staff at their new home, "When we went to Albany, the domestic staff in the Mansion was troubled because they felt they could not cater adequately for us. For instance they had always had to make monumental desserts for the Smiths and thought we would expect even grander dishes. They were greatly relieved when they learned that we ate very simple food like our traditional scrambled eggs for Sunday night suppers."

Eleanor was happy for her husband that he had come back from a devastating illness and won a remarkable victory as the Governor of the largest state in the country. For herself though she was concerned how his new role would affect her but she was determined to continue her independent work and associations that meant so much to her. She would continue her teaching at the Todhunter School, a private girls school in Manhattan. Her son Elliott wrote years later. "The company of her own sex, the compliant students and the appreciative teaching staff had an irresistible appeal to her. It proved she was capable of leading a separate satisfying experience of her own, with no need to lean on Father, Granny or anyone else."

Eleanor developed a schedule to depart Albany for New York for three nights every Sunday evening and return after her 11:00 class on Wednesday morning. Years later she wrote in her book *This I Remember*, "it was a foolish thing for me to have done... I did not have much time to make real friends or see much of the Albany people outside of the official routine. There were many interesting people in the government circle there and some old inhabitants, most of them charming and interesting people of Dutch ancestry with traditions and attachments which went far back into Hudson River history whom I should like to have known better."

## Building His Own Team

One of the first tasks for the new Governor was to build a staff to help him govern the state. Since Al Smith had questioned Roosevelt's physical stamina, he was expecting to maintain some influence in the Governor's office through two of his top aides, Belle Moskowitz and Robert Moses. Both were hoping to stay on in key roles. Eleanor had worked with Moskowitz on Smith's political campaigns and she admired her. However, Eleanor was clear in telling her husband that Moskowitz would be viewed as a Smith person and she would have too much influence if she stayed on. Franklin wanted to choose his own secretary to the Governor and not take Moskowitz. He chose Guernsey Cross, a state assemblyman and former All American basketball player at Cornell, to be his personal assistant.

Franklin did not like Moses who had previously rejected an effort to appoint Louis Howe to a state parks board. He did not want him as a key staff person though he retained him as Chairman of the New York State Council of Parks (1924-1963).

The new Governor had his own inner circle that was led by Louis Howe and included his counsel, Sam Rosenman, party leader James Farley, his neighbor Henry Morgenthau plus his secretary "Missy" LeHand and of course Eleanor. He had an African American valet Irwin McDuffie. Gus Gennerich was his bodyguard. He also personally assisted Roosevelt moving around. Earl Miller, a former state trooper, was assigned to Eleanor and they developed a close personal relationship. Malvina "Tommy" Thompson was Eleanor's personal secretary and key assistant in Albany and later. He chose Edward Flynn, the head of the Bronx Democratic Party, for the key role which Moses had as Secretary of State.

Al Smith resented that FDR didn't keep Robert Moses and Belle Moskowitz and he became increasingly irritated that Roosevelt never asked for his advice.

Eleanor felt that her husband and Smith were very different and had little in common personally other than having a shared commitment to progressive policies. "I was not greatly surprised when after his (Smith's) defeat it became evident that he thought he was going to retain a behind the scenes leadership in the state. It would not work - and he soon discovered that it would not work and left Albany for New York City....That ended the close relationship between my husband and Governor Smith, though there was no open break, so far as I know."

While Roosevelt and Smith would remain friends, their days of being political allies were over. In the years to come, they would become politically competitive and part ways on many issues and policies, especially during Roosevelt's presidency when Smith who went into the business world became an opponent of New Deal policies.

One who worked for Smith who not only remained but was promoted by Roosevelt was Frances Perkins. With her prominence in fighting for the rights of workers after the Triangle Shirtwaist factory fire, Smith later appointed her a member of the state Industrial Board. Roosevelt then appointed her as the Industrial Commissioner, the first woman to head a state agency. She led 1800 employees at a time when many men had never had a female boss and were not comfortable with her at the helm of the department. For Roosevelt, she would lead the state agency to provide worker safety, a minimum wage law, unemployment insurance and reducing the work week for women to 48 hours.

Though she had a close relationship with Smith she was a more low key leader who was trusted so much by Roosevelt that she went with him to Washington when he became President and played a key role in the social and economic policies that Roosevelt enacted in Albany and later in Washington.

As Governor, Roosevelt read up to eight papers in the morning while in bed at the mansion, "propped up with pillows against the Victorian headboard, a white, hand-knit sweater pulled over his pajamas," as the *New York Times* described his routine a few years later. He paid special attention to the editorial pages. He dictated 25 or 30 letters and then made his way to the Capitol where he began to meet scheduled visitors around 11:oo am. Most citizens had no idea how difficult it was for Roosevelt to get around. Photographs of him getting in and out of vehicles were discouraged and he rarely was seen not standing with a crutch or on the arm of his son or an aide.

Frances Perkins related a story about a meeting that evidenced Roosevelt's good will and charm. "About a hundred of us, including many strangers to the Governor, were in the room as he came in leaning on the arm of Guernsey Cross. In the other hand, he carried a stout stick. In those days, he did not walk so well as later. It was but natural common courtesy for those in the room to rise and wait until the Governor reached his desk. It took him a long, long time to reach the desk. The tenseness in the audience grew as it waited in dread, wondering if he would make it. Painfully, slowly and awkwardly, he walked along with Guernsey Cross. It seemed like a terribly long distance. About halfway to the desk, he realized the tension of the audience. He began to smile and nod, tossing his head up gaily. He waved the cane, saying cheerfully, 'That's all right. I will make it.' That was the charm of the man."

## FDR and Radio: The New Medium of the 1920s

Roosevelt became famous for his presidential fireside chats on the radio during the Depression years. He had first successfully used the radio though to communicate with the public as Governor to rally support for his initiatives. Radio was a new medium in the 1920s. For the first time, there was a network of stations to hear the live voice of government leaders. Roosevelt's first radio address as Governor was broadcast from Schenectady station WGY on April 3, 1929. Over his four years as Governor, FDR delivered 39 radio addresses and 29 were aired on WGY which was W for Wireless, G for General Electric where the station was based and Y for Schenectady.

The major newspapers in the state were considered to be conservative and not as supportive of his plans. Roosevelt viewed radio as a way to communicate directly with the people all across the state. He had an appealing and pleasing manner of speaking, even folksy. He used the radio as a means of educating the public about the operations and issues of state government and rallying support for his initiatives.

Eleanor Roosevelt felt that Franklin's ability to communicate with the public was a "gift from God." Describing his speaking ability in her autobiography *This I Remember,* she noted, "His voice lent itself remarkably to the radio. It was a natural gift, for in his whole life, he never had a lesson in diction or public speaking...His voice unquestionably helped him to make the people of the country feel they were an intelligent and understanding part of every government undertaking during his administration."

Frances Perkins also noted his common touch with people, "When he talked on the radio, he saw them in the little parlor, listening with their neighbors. His voice and his facial expression were that of an intimate friend."

In that first radio address in April 1929 he recounted the results of the legislative session and talked about how it was important to use the legislative process so that individual lawmakers could study, understand and debate issues rather than just vote on bills that they had not been given enough time to read.

## The Legislative Session

Once the legislative session began, FDR ran into the opposition of the Republican controlled legislature despite his appeals to put partisanship aside. He intended to fight them when necessary through his use of radio and extensive outreach to rural areas. He had James Farley set up a media office to deliver information to upstate media.

The constitutional amendment passed by the voters in 1927 gave the Governor the power to submit a budget proposal to the Legislature. However, Republican leaders immediately clashed with Roosevelt over control of the process. This clash endured throughout the legislative session. They wanted equal representation on panels to decide spending which Roosevelt put in lump sum categories in his budget.

Roosevelt was considered very affable and friendly to everyone and some questioned whether he was tough enough for the job. As Kenneth Davis wrote in his book about Roosevelt's New York years, "It (Albany) had harsh dissonances and conflicts built into its very structure. And to master it, charm, fortitude, perseverance, hard work and the courtesy of an unusually kind and sensitive man, though helpful, were not enough. He faced a long series of the toughest kind of adversary proceedings in which his opponents would be coldly ambitious men incapable of the finer vibrations committed wholly to organized selfishness, and ruthlessly determined to knock him down."

The Republicans wanted to have a three person committee, the two Republican legislative leaders and the Governor, to determine where that lump sum money went. Roosevelt interpreted the constitution as giving him control of the budget. The Republican legislature proceeded to pass a budget creating their own lump sums and Roosevelt vetoed it. The Republicans sued but the Court of Appeals decided in the Governor's favor, a ruling that set a precedent that continues to this day.

Once the legislative session ended in April, Roosevelt was off to Warm Springs, Georgia for three weeks to continue his therapy. While there he made a number of speeches to various groups including the Atlanta Bar Association, a college commencement, and a beef cattle show. Like all governors he was a cheerleader for the state and in remarks broadcast back to the state from Warm Springs he extolled New York's natural beauty and famous lakes and mountains and seacoasts. He encouraged New Yorkers and those from across the country to visit New York. By hand, he wrote in his typed remarks that Lake Placid would be hosting the Winter Olympics in 1932.

During and after the legislative session he made speeches to numerous groups in the state on the usual host of subjects that Governors discuss about the programs and services of the state. He spoke at conferences about agriculture, health care, prisons, waterpower, good government and even morals and his ideas about the state.

On April 8th, extra state troopers were assigned to the Governor's Mansion after a bomb addressed to the Governor was discovered at the New York post office and Eleanor Roosevelt was very upset. The *New York Times* reported, "The Governor showed a tendency to treat the bomb episode as a joke, but his wife was understood to have asked for special police protection not only here (Albany) but at their homes in Hyde Park and New York.

Eleanor's fears did not extend to airplanes. On June 5th, two years after Charles Lindbergh's famous non-stop flight to Paris she made her first flight in an airplane. It was a six passenger, 300 horsepower plane designed to be a "flying laboratory" for observation and experimentation. Eleanor named the plane, "The Governor" and poured a bottle of ginger ale to christen its propeller. She took a twenty minute flight from Albany's municipal airport and went over Albany, Schenectady and Troy. Then, she took her second flight to New York City but the pilot brought the plane down in Poughkeepsie because of a threatened storm with lightning. She took a train to New York from there and was very happy with her experience. This time, her usually unflappable husband was anxious when he did not hear from her until he was informed that she had arrived in New York.

In June 1929 Governor Roosevelt gave the commencement addresses and received honorary degrees at Hobart, Fordham and Harvard where his classmates were having their 25th reunion and he was chosen to lead a parade.

At Fordham University, a Jesuit Catholic university, he used the occasion to spell out his religious and spiritual views and discussed them in the context of the state's motto "Excelsior." He noted that a friend from another state thought this motto connoted a feeling of superiority.

Roosevelt said he didn't feel New York State should feel superior because of its great metropolis and leadership in industry and agriculture, but that the word was appropriate in a different, spiritual context,

"To live up to that great motto in its right interpretation should be the goal of our state. To think of that motto in its spiritual aspect, to think of it in connection with our duty to our fellow-men, to think of it in the light of the Golden Rule, will mean that the twelve million people who by the grace of God chance to be citizens of one human political unit known as the State of New York, will in the days to come measure up more widely and more truly to the highest teachings of religion and to the best purposes of our American civilization."

On July 9, he spoke to students at Syracuse University about state government and noted how he estimated it had become ten times more than what it was fifty years earlier in 1880 when it had only two functions, prisons and institutions for people in need who couldn't take care of themselves.

He told the students, "In the past fifty years the State has undertaken a great number of additional social activities such for instance, as the care and instruction of the deaf, the teaching of the blind, the maintenance of a great institution for our tubercular cases, another great institution for the treatment of cancer and kindred diseases and also a hospital and home for crippled children."

He talked about other facilities using language that was common at the time but very politically incorrect today, "hospitals and schools for the mentally deficient as distinguished from the insane. Here the state is caring for thousands of children who in popular language would be called morons and we are accomplishing great things in educating them to be sufficiently normal to go out in the communities and lead useful individual lives."

In his first summer as Governor, Roosevelt was confronted with the kind of major crisis that falls in the lap of governors when there are life threatening problems at facilities run by state agencies. Overcrowded and even inhumane state prison conditions led to violent riots at facilities in Dannemora in northern New York and Auburn with the deaths of inmates as well as guards. Roosevelt decided to set up a commission to study prison overcrowding, work programs and other issues at the prisons.

## Touring the State

As Governor, Franklin Roosevelt liked to spend the summer months touring the state often in his car but also he went along the Erie Canal by boat. He liked to visit local communities and state facilities along the way. These were often inspection tours. Eleanor went with him and she was his eyes and ears since he could not walk through the facilities easily. She described the meetings in *This I Remember* by writing, "The head of the institution that we were visiting usually got into the car with my husband and drove around the grounds, pointing out what new buildings were needed and where they would be built." Eleanor would go inside many of the state facilities with questions. He would tell her to check everything out. She recounted, "At first my reports were highly unsatisfactory to him. I would tell him what was on the menu for the day and he would ask, 'Did you look to see whether the inmates actually were getting that food'?" So, she learned to check mattresses and closets and look under the tops of kettles on the stove.

Roosevelt saw that many state institutions were overcrowded and facilities outdated. As a result of his tours he would propose major spending increases to upgrade facilities and build new ones.

The Governor knew the state had a small boat for canal inspections, *The Inspector,* and he decided to use it that first summer when he toured the Erie Canal and later traveled by boat down the St. Lawrence River to Montreal. Roosevelt was bullish on waterpower and the future of the North Country which he viewed as having the opportunity to become "another Pittsburgh." He talked about building a bridge across the St. Lawrence River near Alexandria Bay and Clayton and he predicted other bridges would be built along the river.

Meanwhile, Eleanor and their two youngest children joined Franklin and would go to Montreal. She and the children, James and Franklin Jr., were leaving on an ocean liner from there and heading for a six week trip to Europe. Her close friends, Nancy Cook and Marion Dickerman, were also joining her for the trip to Ireland, England, Wales, and Belgium. On the night before their departure Franklin gave them a bon voyage party at the Mount Royal Hotel in Montreal.

Governor Roosevelt then returned to New York State by taking canals in Canada down Lake Champlain to Whitehall, Lake George and down the Hudson River to Albany.

Later in the summer when he arrived at the State Fair in Syracuse on August 29, he remarked on his tours, "For two months I have spent the greater part of the time visiting different parts of the State of New York and the fact that I have traveled nearly six thousand miles and visited almost every county proves that we have a real empire within our state." He spoke at the fair about agricultural and rural policies and how the State had equalized the tax burden in the state. The legislation though was only effective as long as passed on by county governments. In a radio address after the tours, he said he had been impressed with state facilities housing those with special needs but he said they were overcrowded and that a major increase in funding was needed to upgrade the facilities.

During another auto tour in September 1929, FDR attended the groundbreaking for a new memorial highway honoring veterans that was being built to near the top of Whiteface Mountain. He also went to see how preparations were progressing in nearby Lake Placid for the 1932 Winter Olympics. A parade was held into the village and Jack Shea, the 19 year old speed skating phenom, showed the governor the new speed skating oval in front of the high school. A picture of the two smiling appeared in the Sunday edition of the *New York Times*. Shea recalled, "He drove up in a big open Packard and with that famous smile and his distinctive cigarette holder." Roosevelt said to him, "Young man, maybe I'll see you here two years from now."

## The Great Depression

In the fall of 1929 Franklin Roosevelt's first term agenda on key issues was turned upside down as the Roaring Twenties came to an end with the Stock Market crash that led to the beginning of the Great Depression. There had been rumblings that after flying high for months, the Stock Market was overextended and due for a significant retraction. The tremors began in late October and the crash came on Tuesday, October 29, 1929. Within weeks millions of persons were out of work. State and local finances were being thrown into shambles. The Roaring Twenties and the fun days of the Jazz Age prosperity were over.

Roosevelt's agenda in Albany had to be completely re-focused on employment, economic relief and the economy. Not only would the economic crisis become a priority for Roosevelt as Governor, it became a defining issue that thrust him into a prominent position as his bold actions gained even more national political attention.

At first Roosevelt did not call for major programs to address the economic collapse since he thought the crisis would be short lived. The stock market recovered somewhat in January and had a rally for several months after President Hoover prevailed on business leaders to take what actions they could to rescue the economy. Roosevelt believed in the free enterprise system and resisted any strong government intervention. Many business leaders also felt they would have to again ride out the ups and downs of the business cycle. President Hoover downplayed the situation too saying, "All the evidence indicates that the worst effects of the crash upon unemployment will have been passed within the next sixty days." He also noted that "prosperity is just around the corner."

Then, in May 1930 the Stock Market began to plunge again. Soup kitchens and bread lines had become a common sight in New York City. At one church soup line, they were stretched out for blocks in midtown close to the site of the new massive skyscraper being built, the Empire State Building.

While Roosevelt's first inclination was not for government action to influence the markets he became the first governor in the country to consider taking action to address unemployment. It was not viewed by many as a function of government to spend money to stimulate the economy and provide jobs for unemployed workers. On March 29, 1930 Roosevelt made the case for government action by drawing a parallel to fighting an epidemic, "The situation is serious and the time has come for us to face this unpleasant fact as dispassionately and constructively as a scientist faces a test tube of deadly germs."

As the situation continued to worsen, Roosevelt became more alarmed by the extent of joblessness and he became convinced that strong action by the government not private industry was needed to address the crisis. He went further and said that the federal government had to help states and localities too. Many people thought the massive number of people unemployed was a failure of capitalism. There was a growing concern after the Bolshevik Revolution in Russia just twelve years earlier that the United States could face a demand by the poor and the unemployed for more government and even socialist control of the economy.

Roosevelt saw the need for legislation to provide public work and unemployment assistance for those who lost their jobs. Republicans still controlled the State Legislature and Roosevelt needed to work with them to come up with legislation to provide relief. Government intervention and support for the economy on such a scale had never happened before but Roosevelt not only felt it was an important humanitarian policy but also would help to revive the economy by putting money in peoples' pockets. He was often criticized for not having firm political policies and principles, but this flexibility was displayed in his willingness to experiment with innovative, new  programs to address the crisis.

## The Empire State and City

The Roosevelts spent Christmas Eve 1929 in Albany at the Executive Mansion before going to Hyde Park on Christmas Day. They started a tradition while in the Governor's mansion,  inviting orphans from the St. Vincent home next to the mansion for a Christmas party.

As a new decade had dawned in 1930 in the midst of the Great Depression, New York City was becoming a modern metropolis. The city had over 10 million residents and in the mid-1920s had become the largest city in the world, surpassing London. Despite the economic calamity facing the country, Franklin Roosevelt presided over a city and state in the midst of the historic construction of New York City's iconic Art Deco skyscrapers. The Chrysler Building opened in 1930 at the corner of 42nd Street and  Lexington Avenue. It was the tallest building in New York City when it was completed on May 27, 1930.

On January 15th, Governor Roosevelt submitted his second executive budget under the new constitutional amendment. His proposed budget was slightly above $311,000,000, an increase of

$46,500,000 from the previous year due to planned increases in prison and hospital construction.

In February Roosevelt delivered a radio address to the public and discussed his budget and programmatic issues. He mentioned a prison riot at the Auburn state prison and talked about the need to rebuild the prisons, some of which were one hundred years old. He also continued to stress the importance of publicly-owned water power which was a major issue especially in the 20th century's early years. This issue remained a priority for him because he wanted to lower rates for electricity for "householders" as electricity was used more and more for "labor saving devices." Electricity was a desired public commodity which revolutionized homes and the way people lived.

Governor Al Smith had first sought to keep the water power potential of the St. Lawrence River on the Canadian border as a public resource to be used to provide affordable electricity for consumers. Many farms and rural areas did not have access to electric power. They used windmills to pump water. Smith wanted to expand rural electrification.

Roosevelt wanted to build a power dam on the St. Lawrence River to generate hydroelectric power. During his summer tours he visited the St. Lawrence region to meet with leaders and look at locations for power development. He proposed the creation of the Power Authority as a public agency that would develop water power. The benefits of public control were hindered by the lack of public transmission lines which were controlled by Hudson Niagara, a monopoly company formed by the merger of three companies.

Roosevelt liked to emphasize that public utilities were granted franchises by the state and these companies should help the entire state and equalize their rates. He stated, "The underlying theory covering all public utilities is that they receive the privilege of a special franchise from the people of the State themselves, and that for this privilege, they must give the best possible service equally to all citizens of the state."

He noted that two thirds of farmhouses had no electricity. "Many of you doubtless know examples as I do of householders who would like to install electricity in their homes and their farms but who feel that the initial cost of the installations is made so high by the electric companies that they are totally unable to afford it." Roosevelt also knew that on the other side of the border in Ontario where the province ran the power facilities that electric rates were substantially less.

Republicans who controlled the State Legislature did not want the state in the business of building transmission lines. Roosevelt used the radio to make a major address in 1930 to support it. He saw it as a winning issue that put Republicans on the defensive because of their support for the big utility companies that were charging rates higher than he felt was needed. While he was criticized by conservatives who opposed state control of power, he was criticized on the left by Socialist Norman Thomas who wanted the state to own the water resources and transmission lines. In his annual address to the Legislature in January, Roosevelt proposed like Thomas that the state own the electrical transmission facilities.

Republicans were furious and didn't want Roosevelt getting an advantage on the issue because they knew that public power was a popular issue. They felt they would not be able to defeat Roosevelt in 1930 if that was a key issue.

Roosevelt was pleased that the Republicans in the Legislature were at least willing to join him in appointing a commission on water power development in the St. Lawrence River. He also complained about telephone rates and wanted the state to have more control over these rates rather than the federal government which controlled interstate commerce.

In late March he gave two radio broadcasts from WABC in New York and from WGY in Schenectady for upstate listeners to push for passage of a $50 million bond issue for construction to modernize state hospitals for those with mental illness.

## — *Old Age Security*

The issue of old age financial security had become more urgent with the onset of the Great Depression. Older persons were often victims of age discrimination in employment. They were increasingly unable to find work during the Depression and few were wealthy enough to have saved money for retirement. Often they were the first to be laid off. Over 50% of older persons lived in poverty conditions. They often were forced to go to the "poorhouse" or almshouse rather than be able to stay in their own homes. Some even were forced to sue their children for support.

There had been a growing movement in the states in the 1920s to enact some kind of retirement income for the older population. The Townsend movement in California sought to enact state legislation for pensions to provide retirement security. Other states had also passed legislation to provide pensions for older persons. The federal government had first enacted pensions for Civil War veterans. In January 1929 as FDR took office, the *Albany Times Union* reported that 35 Albany area widows of Civil War veterans would be getting $10 more each month if a bill in Congress was passed.

The issue had been a priority for social welfare organizations in New York State too. Roosevelt wanted to act on the issue which he had promoted during his election campaign. He wanted a plan that included contributions by workers and employers rather than just outright financial support that would put workers on "the dole." He felt that providing direct relief would make the program seem like an extension of the welfare system.

He called for legislation first that would create a commission to study the issues and make a recommendation for legislative action. That bill passed in 1929 and a commission was formed. Advocates then sought to influence the commission as well as legislators and the Governor who received hundreds of letters which poured into his office in support of the concept. Petition drives were started with lists of signatories sent to the Governor.

The American Association for Old Age Security was a national organization pushing the concept across the country and it was very active in the advocacy campaign in New York. Roosevelt received a letter from one man who was a New York resident visiting in Louisiana, "I am eighty years of age with no means of support, my sons fought in France during the world war and two are dead as a result. I am now visiting here with one and would like to return to my old home soon. Please advise me if such a law has been enacted and if it has been please send an application to fill out."

Another letter from upstate said, "I am writing you for information, as to what will be necessary to procure such help for an aunt born and a life-long resident of N.Y. state who is eighty five years old, blind, deaf and without a cent in the world to call her own. We have cared for her since she was stricken blind over a year ago (Apr. 1928) and would gladly continue to do so, but for the fact, that matters have gone so hardly with us here on the farm, that we will be hard put to it, to get our school tax together this year and to avoid doing that, which, to her is horrible (Place her on the town.) and to us. I am writing to you personally for this information. Thank you in advance and with every best wish for a Merry Christmas and Happy new year to you and your family."

At a hearing on March 11, 1930, 200 persons representing 50 organizations attended. Catholic and Protestant organizations supported the bill along with labor unions and social services advocates. Socialists said the bill did not go far enough and opposed it. They wanted an amendment to the state constitution establishing a pension system run by state government. The New York State Real Estate Board opposed it because of its effect on taxes and denounced the "theory that the state owes everyone a living." Dr. Stephen Wise, rabbi of the Free Synagogue in New York City jousted with the representative of the Real Estate Board who had also suggested that supporters read about the French Revolution "to see the effects of taxing the middle class out of existence." Dr. Wise replied, "It was such views as yours that made it necessary to have a revolution to get justice." Wise went on, "Once the aged workman was common. Now, industry has scrapped the man of 70, 60 and even 50."

The commission came back with a proposal to enact a new pension program and the Assembly passed it unanimously. After Senate passage, Governor Roosevelt signed the old age security bill on April 10, 1930 to provide the pensions for the "needy" age 70 or older. The pensions would be available on January 1, 1931 and would average $242 a year for about 51,000 persons. The cost would be $12.5 million annually to be divided by the state and the counties. The Governor said at the bill signing, "One of the things that delights my soul was that my party platform on which I was nominated two years ago called for the legislation to provide old age security."

While the Governor extolled the bill in front of 250 persons and representatives of advocacy organizations, he said, "I am a little bit disappointed because it is too much a mere extension of the poor law. It will give the aged food and a roof over their heads, but I had hoped it would provide more. My hope is that some day we can have a system to encourage savings that will provide ease and comfort as well as food and shelter." He added that other countries were far ahead in old age security and he hoped that the law would be improved the following year.

In April the Governor gave an address on the Accomplishments and Failures of the 1930 Session. He listed fourteen specific actions accomplished topped by improving the care of prisoners and creating a Parole Board, changing state banking powers, and enacting an Old Age Security law.

Regarding failures, he criticized the Legislature for failing to abide by a proposal to modernize local government and to create non-partisan election boards. His most pointed remarks were directed at the failure on the public utility issue saying, "A better illustration of the weak leadership of the majority could not be found." He also specifically mentioned several bills which the Legislature did not enact including an eight day and forty hour week for women in industry, an Advisory Fair Wage Board for women and children and the Anti-Monopoly law.

He said he was giving his report not to give himself any credit, "The record speaks for itself and credit should be given where it is due."

Roosevelt's progressive legislative successes had already gained him wide attention as a prospective Presidential candidate in 1932. On June 30, he went to the National Governors Association meeting in Salt Lake City and made a presentation discussing unemployment and old age pensions. He saw the problem that as people aged, employers no longer wanted them and they ended up institutionalized in poorhouses. He wanted to give them dignity. "Up to the present time most of us have been thinking of old age insurance in terms of the very old and in terms of the old-fashioned almshouse, poor house or county farm. Today, however, old age security logically and inevitably ties in with the whole problem of the unemployed. The reason is, first, that when old men and old women are no longer able to support themselves by working they come into the ranks of the unemployed just as much as if they were the victims of industrial layoffs. The only difference is that their lay-off is permanent rather then temporary. The other reason is the tendency of the speeded-up American industrial machine to decline to employ men and women who have merely reached middle age and have not yet reached real old age."

He again proposed what for the time was a very progressive and proactive approach by the federal government. He wanted a national program enacted that would not just be an extension of welfare but would include payroll contributions by workers. He said the New York State law "takes only one short step toward the larger problem...

It has set up no machinery for the building for what in time must become an insurance fund to which the state and the workers, and possibly the employer, will contribute."

Poorhouses across the country began to close as this direct pension aid was provided to older persons in several states. The concept of Social Security was already in his mind and five years later, he would sign the law to enact it as President.

## A Hero's Welcome

On June 24, 1930, Governor Roosevelt welcomed to Albany an old friend, Admiral Richard Byrd, and nine others in his party who had just returned a week earlier from the first flight over the South Pole. It was a highly anticipated mission, widely followed by the public. Byrd had previously flown over the North Pole. Byrd arrived by a destroyer after a ten hour voyage up the Hudson River from New York and was greeted all along the banks of the river by enthusiastic large crowds at Poughkeepsie, Kingston, Saugerties and Castleton. Following his safe return a week earlier, 50,000 people jammed the streets of Albany and around the Capitol as Governor Roosevelt on the second level of steps on the Capitol gave Byrd the state's gold medal which had only been given to Charles Lindbergh.

The *New York Times* reported, "The city greeted them with shrill whistles of boats and factories and blasts of locomotives on the banks of the Hudson, sent them slowly up State Street, through solid masses of cheering people and presented them in the midst of crowded Capitol Park to Governor Roosevelt for the conferring of the Distinguished Service Medal of the State."

Roosevelt called Byrd "one of my oldest and best of friends," and recalled their days when he was the Assistant Secretary of the Navy and

Byrd was a Junior Lieutenant and they used to spend night after night discussing philosophy in a hunting camp in New Brunswick.

In July Roosevelt, Eleanor, and his secretary Missy LeHand went to Newington, Connecticut to join Governor Trumbull to dedicate a new hospital for disabled children. Speaking at the dedication, Eleanor said, "We are fortunate to be living in an age when modern methods may aid our afflictions. Fifty years ago we would not have been able to get off our backs because then there were no fine modern hospitals and infirmaries such as this beautiful and well equipped building we are dedicating this afternoon."

Governor Roosevelt called a special session in August after an eighteen day tour of state facilities. As the economic crisis deepened he searched for more ways to address it, accepting the need for experiments and he saw government as the means to make positive changes in peoples' lives.

## The Re-Election Campaign of 1930

Franklin Roosevelt was looking forward to his 1930 campaign for re-election. In those years, the gubernatorial term was just two years. Not only did he feel he had done a good job for the state, but the Great Depression had politically weakened the entire Republican party. Roosevelt enjoyed campaigning and he again traveled around the state in the fall of 1930.

While he had only squeaked by to win in 1928, his radio addresses and travels around the state had increased his popularity. Roosevelt's policies were also viewed favorably during his first two years in office. He had won the support of farmers, older persons, labor and those who opposed Prohibition. He also continued to promote his plan for lower electricity prices particularly as he noted the cheaper cost of electricity across the state's northern border in Canada where the government owned the hydroelectric power plants and transmission facilities. His re-election drive was even dubbed the "waffle iron" campaign as he talked about the everyday household uses of electricity and made the issue a major focus.

Since he was first elected, the Great Depression had changed the economic outlook in the country and there was a strong political tide against the Republican Party and President Hoover. Roosevelt had also sought to take action to help people deal with the economic impact of the Depression with the legislation for old age pensions and emergency work relief programs.

Roosevelt viewed himself as a man who grew up in a rural area and was knowledgeable and he had actively supported efforts to improve conservation and agriculture.

Roosevelt had also gained the active support of organized labor with his efforts on old age pensions, the minimum wage and unemployment. He was endorsed by the State Labor Federation. Roosevelt established a warm, working relationship with career civil servants early in his term. Their employee organization, the Association of State Civil Service Employees (later the CSEA) had no formal bargaining rights or recognition status at that time. Roosevelt tacitly recognized them by attending their annual dinner meeting and maintaining a friendly and cooperative exchange of correspondence.

His Republican opponent, Charles Tuttle, the US Attorney for the Southern District of New York, was a clear underdog. Tuttle and the Republicans planned to make corruption of Tammany Hall as the main issue in the campaign. Tuttle hammered away, charging Roosevelt had not been aggressive in dealing with corruption.

While Roosevelt's party in New York City was run by Tammany Hall and Roosevelt had appointed persons supported by Tammany, he also had an independent image and had fought Tammany as a reformer in the past. Roosevelt was viewed as honest and not part of the shenanigans of the party. Voters also knew that Republican political machines ran upstate counties and that the Republican Party had been responsible for the Teapot Dome bribery scandal in Washington just a few years earlier.

Still, Roosevelt was concerned that the Tammany situation could cut into his winning margin. If he didn't win by an overwhelming margin, it could hurt him in 1932 when other candidates might not view him as the frontrunner.

Meanwhile, Republicans were worried that a big Roosevelt victory would make him the likely Democratic Presidential nominee in 1932. His re-election in New York would be a significant threat to President Hoover who dispatched Secretary of State Henry Stimson to issue a radio address from Washington saying Roosevelt was unfit for office because he was presiding over judicial scandals of Tammany Hall and failed to address them. Republicans also said the Democrats were ignoring the fact that the United States, under Hoover, was suffering from the Depression less than other nations.

Roosevelt was glad to discuss the Depression and he campaigned across the state, attacking the Republicans and their Wall Street allies for causing the economic collapse. He also continually charged that Tuttle was straddling the Prohibition issue in an effort to try to appeal to some who were opposed to it.

Roosevelt accepted his re-nomination at the state convention in Syracuse in October with his mother Sara, wife, Eleanor and daughter Anna attending. Former Governor Al Smith returned to the convention and got a warm welcome and applause for his remarks.

In his acceptance speech Roosevelt argued, "that progressive government, by its very terms, must be a living and a growing thing, that the battle for it is never ending and that if we let up for one single moment or one single year, not merely do we stand still but we fall back in the march of civilization."

Roosevelt's personal campaign appearances were supplemented by a strong ground campaign that included a naturalized citizens bureau that did outreach to 28 different national groups. The campaign also produced "talking movies" with Roosevelt, Al Smith and others that were a big hit, especially upstate.

In a closing speech in the campaign at Carnegie Hall in Manhattan, Roosevelt attacked the Republicans, "Now we have come to the close of the campaign, I ask the electorate of the State of New York for their support. I ask this as a rebuke to these Republican national and state leaders who, substituting false charges and deliberate misrepresentations, have had the cowardice to ignore the great problems and issues before the whole state."

In the end, despite Tuttle's efforts to drag Roosevelt down with the Tammany Hall mess, the overriding issue was the Great Depression and Tuttle could not overcome the mood of voters nationally to punish the Republicans for allowing the speculation and greed on Wall Street that led to the economic collapse that damaged so many lives.

On Election Day 1930 Franklin Roosevelt easily exceeded his narrow victory in 1928 with the largest landslide in state history, whipping Tuttle by 725,000, almost doubling Al Smith's 386,000 vote record victory in 1922. Roosevelt won over 56% of the vote to Tuttle's 34% with minor parties getting the rest. Roosevelt carried over forty counties in typically Republican upstate rural areas and won the vote in upstate New York by nearly 168,000. He won the Town of Potsdam for the first time since 1860 and Chautauqua County went Democrat for the first time since Grover Cleveland won as Governor in 1882. Republican control of the State Legislature was weakened. They lost seats in the State Senate and had only a one seat majority after the election while the Assembly had 80 Republicans and 70 Democrats.

Nationally, Democrats took control of the House of Representatives for the first time since 1916 and were one seat away from parity in the Senate. The Democratic Party was on the move and Franklin Roosevelt's New York landslide made him the favorite for the Presidency in 1932.

When the Roosevelts returned to Albany on the 12:50 pm train from New York they were met by throngs in the streets turned out by the Albany Democratic party despite a rainstorm. The *New York Times* described the scene: "Down Albany's Broadway the parade went with many following afoot and a police escort having a hard time keeping enthusiasts off the car. Windows of buildings along the line of the march were filled with people who waved a friendly greeting and hurled ticker tape and colored strings of paper which floated down amid the rain. Up State Street and the buildings were thronged and as the parade pushed ahead in the driving storm a steady roar of exploding bombs, automobile horns and cheers hailed the successful candidate."

The procession finally made its way to the Governor's mansion on Eagle Street and a large crowd was there on the lawn and gave the Governor and Eleanor a big cheer when they appeared. Roosevelt told them "You people in Albany did me proud."

## Second Term

Following Franklin Roosevelt's overwhelming re-election victory and his progressive economic policies to address the high unemployment caused by the Great Depression, he had clearly emerged as the leading contender for the Democratic Presidential nomination in 1932. By early 1931, many thought his nomination was more than likely given that he was the Governor of the nation's largest state and his name was Roosevelt.

Like many ambitious governors and politicians then and now, Roosevelt claimed he was only focused on his job as Governor. However, not long after the election in November, he asked Ed Flynn, the Bronx Borough President and Secretary of State to stay at the Governor's mansion. That night Roosevelt told Flynn and Louis Howe that he thought he could win the Democratic nomination in 1932. He had already quietly asked his campaign manager, James Farley, to lead an effort to reach out to key Democrats around the country to talk about Roosevelt's accomplishments in New York. In fact, when Roosevelt first took office in 1929, Farley and Louis Howe had been sending mail to prominent Democrats from Roosevelt asking their thoughts about the future course for the party.

After his re-election, a Friends of Roosevelt committee began soliciting money from wealthy donors like Joseph P. Kennedy. The Democrats were eager for a victory in 1932 because only two Democrats, Grover Cleveland and Woodrow Wilson, had been elected President since 1856.

Roosevelt was inaugurated for a second, two-year term as Governor on January 2, 1931 in the Assembly chamber in Albany. The whole family, Eleanor, his mother Sara, and his children James and his wife, Anna and her husband, Elliott, Franklin Jr and John, were all in the chamber for the festivities which included again a 19 gun salute in Capitol Park after the oath of office was administered and a reception held later at the mansion.

The ceremony only took 45 minutes and at Roosevelt's request the events were scaled back with a military parade canceled and expenses far less than previous years because of the austerity during the Depression. Roosevelt had invited Democrats from across the country as well as those from the state but there were some empty seats in the chamber.

Roosevelt used his inaugural address to call for the modernization of local government which he said had become ineffective and been controlled by local politics, "It is my ardent hope that in the twenty years to come, the people of New York will be able to accomplish as much for the cause of improved local government along American lines as we have accomplished in our state government in the past twenty years."

A few days later he made his annual address to the Legislature.

In 1931 the Legislature approved a bill limiting the work week for women and children to six days and 48 hours per week. However, a minimum wage bill was resisted because higher costs might force industry to leave the state.

Roosevelt took steps to exert leadership in addressing the Depression. Further enhancing his national profile, he called a regional meeting of states in the Northeast to come up with joint solutions to the economic situation with the governors of Massachusetts, Rhode Island, Connecticut, New Jersey, Pennsylvania and Ohio. The governors met in Albany on January 23 to consider unemployment and social welfare relief programs and to agree to study facts and methods of relief in the United States and in other countries.

The State Business Council opposed the idea of increased government spending and wanted 10% across the board cuts in state government to close its budget gap. Roosevelt opposed the cuts though and noted that the average salary for the 31,000 state workers was just over $1500 annually and almost half had an annual salary of $818.

There were nearly two million persons out of work in New York State and an emergency appropriation was exhausted two months before the previous November 15 when it was supposed to expire. Roosevelt then proposed a $30 million bond issue for unemployment that was approved by the voters. Roosevelt felt it was the obligation of state government to "prevent starvation or the want of any of its fellow men or women who try to maintain themselves but cannot."

Eleanor Roosevelt noted, "It was part of Franklin's political philosophy - and over and over again I heard him expound it - that the great benefit to be derived from having forty-eight states was the possibility of experimenting on a small scale to see how a program worked before trying it out nationally."

He claimed the crisis was national and beyond the ability of New York to respond so he said the federal government needed to bail out the states with national relief programs. "It becomes the positive duty of the government to step in," he said.

The Legislature passed a bill in the session creating the state Power Authority and Roosevelt signed it in April 1931. This was a major step toward public control of water resources especially in the St. Lawrence River. President Hoover, already keeping an eye on Roosevelt regarding the 1932 Presidential race, attempted to cut the state out of the issue by negotiating a treaty directly with Canada.

After the legislative session ended, FDR and his son Elliot took off for Paris in May to visit his mother who was ill at the American hospital there and then they sailed back from Cherbourg.

1931 also saw the continuing growth of New York City as a futuristic metropolis. In May the Chrysler Building was surpassed as the tallest building eleven months after it opened by a structure that would symbolize the city in the early and mid 20th century. The Empire State Building was completed and Roosevelt attended the dedication of the building on May 1, 1931. It was the largest building in the world, a stunning Art Deco edifice that was futuristic at the time. President Hoover was there to switch on the lights for the first time. No one had ever seen New York from that vantage point, 86 floors above the ground where people and cars looked like insects.

This event brought Roosevelt together again with Al Smith who had taken a job as the general manager of the building. Smith remarked, "The state of New York can use this building anytime it wants to. The governor can have a meeting up here and if the session lasts into the warm weather, he can bring the thirty day bills up on the roof here and we will provide him with lemonade and he can dispose of the state's business at the highest point on the continent."

Governor Roosevelt talked about the dramatic view, "I am still a little awestruck. I have not got my new sense of proportion back yet. I have got an entirely new conception of things in the city of New York. As a simple countryman who has only been here in New York for twenty five years, I still think of things in terms of fields and creeks. And, when I looked out north and saw Central Park, it reminded me of the sides of my cow pasture in Hyde Park."

On July 23 Governor Roosevelt met with Chicago Mayor Anton Cermak at the Governor's home in New York. Then, he began his annual summer tour of the state by visiting Jones Beach on Long Island and attended a luncheon with Democratic officials including former Governor Smith. The following week he visited state institutions in Rockland County.

Fearing the economic situation would worsen in the winter of 1931-32, Roosevelt did not want to wait until the new legislative session in January to propose new programs. So in August 1931 he called a special session of the Legislature and was given the authority and funding to address unemployment relief. A $20 million appropriation to create a new Temporary Emergency Relief Agency (TERA) was approved. Funding would come from a 50% increase in the state income tax and he called for those "who have benefitted by our industrial and economic system to come to the front in such a grave emergency and assist those who under the same industrial and economic order are the losers and sufferers. I believe their contribution should be in proportion to the benefits they receive and the prosperity they enjoy."

When TERA was created, Roosevelt selected Macy's President Jesse Straus as its President. Straus then appointed Harry Hopkins to run the new agency. Hopkins was a social worker who oversaw nonprofit agencies and programs. He had been appointed by New York City Mayor John Purroy Mitchel as Executive Secretary of the Bureau of Child Welfare. Hopkins eventually became the President of the agency. Hopkins would stay with Roosevelt as one of his top aides to oversee the Federal Emergency Relief Administration (FERA) when he moved on to the White House.

TERA provided government paid jobs for 160,000 New Yorkers who were unemployed and had been citizens of New York for two years prior to November 1, 1931. One aspect of it was conservation work. Roosevelt always had a keen interest in conservation and the environment. He enjoyed growing up and living in the Hudson Valley and roaming around his family's estate which his mother had put under his control in 1910. As a State Senator at that time he served as Chair of the Conservation Committee. TERA recruited a "tree army" to plant 10,000 trees across the state to prevent erosion and to sustain the timber industry in the future. This project would in part be a forerunner for the Civilian Conservation Corps (CCC) which FDR quickly created by an Executive Order after he became President.

In the fall when Roosevelt was back in Warm Springs, he was having a hard time trying to downplay his presidential aspirations in 1932 though he was certainly planning to run and was expected to by many political leaders across the country. 2000 people attended a barbecue in Warm Springs in October at which Roosevelt insisted, "This is not a political gathering. It is just a neighborly gathering and I speak sincerely when I say that it touches me deeply." The barbecue was organized by the Roosevelt for President Club of Meriwether County, which was honoring him as a Warm Springs neighbor but also as the next President of the United States. A representative of 50 Roosevelt for President clubs from Alabama also attended the barbecue. From Atlanta he took a train to Virginia to participate in the 150th anniversary of the surrender of Cornwallis at Yorktown marking the end of the Revolutionary War.

Later in the month Governor Roosevelt was back in New York on October 24, 1931 to help dedicate another new engineering landmark. Roosevelt joined his fellow New Jersey Governor Morgan Foster Larson to dedicate the George Washington Bridge, a span that connected the two states and has endured to this day. 5000 people attended the ceremony but the *New York Times* reported that another 20,000 were on the sides of the bridge. In his remarks Roosevelt said, "In 1931, we may still regard as a peace-time triumph, evidence that our nation is aware that both individual prosperity and civic well--being depend on mutual aid. As an example of constructive cooperation between two great states, this bridge is worthy of its name."

A few days later on October 27 Roosevelt was delighted to preside at a special public event for the new Theodore Roosevelt Memorial on Central Park in New York. "Of all the public events in which, as Governor, I have been privileged to participate during the past three years, I am very certain that this laying of the cornerstone of the Roosevelt Memorial thrills and interests me the most. It is in part because of my long association with the Museum. My memory goes back to a day 37 years ago, when a small boy of twelve marched proudly up the steps of the old brick building which formed the nucleus of what would become the great American Museum of Natural History of today. It was not long after this that Theodore Roosevelt, hearing that my Grandfather had given me a life membership in the Museum, said to me, 'Franklin, you can learn more about nature and life in the Museum than in all the books and schools in the world'."

The Roosevelts returned again to Warm Springs for Thanksgiving and at the annual dinner at Warm Springs he called for more aid for those suffering from polio and for a new extension service to reach others across the country. He wanted to spread the "gospel of Warm Springs that infantile paralysis can and will be conquered" as he said in his remarks. He noted that in New York state there were 6500 new cases in New York State in 1931. (In 1938 he founded the National Foundation for Infantile Paralysis known as the the March of Dimes).

While in Georgia, Eleanor spoke about world peace to the Atlanta League of Women Voters at a luncheon given in her honor, saying that men "for traditional reasons are not going to do much about war.... any successful crusade against it must be conducted by women of all countries....Nationals must come together not in fear but in trust and step by step, the world may be led to settle disputes in a more civilized way." And she called for women to be more active in government, "The more you study government the more you realize it is quite impossible to sit back and criticize and not do anything."

As the Christmas season approached the Governor again made an appeal to buy Christmas seals to benefit the fight against tuberculosis, another disease that continued to be a public health concern. On the two days before Christmas the Governor again hosted two parties for over 100 children from the St. Vincent's Orphan Asylum and gave them gifts. On Christmas Eve, all of the family arrived in Albany to spend Christmas Day at the Governor's Mansion and then went to Hyde Park for the weekend.

## 1932: The Decisive Year

As the legislative session opened in Albany at the dawn of the 1932 presidential election year, Roosevelt delivered a dramatic message, a call to arms to the State Legislature on January 6. It was a message for New Yorkers but it exuded the sweeping rhetoric of national leadership and the context of history as he compared those who fought in the Great War to those struggling to survive the Depression. Unlike the previous year when he did not focus on the unemployed, he emphatically stated, "To those millions who now starve we owe a duty as sacred as to those thousands who died in France, to see to it that this shall not come again. This is the duty of all of us, leaders in business, finance, agriculture, labor and government."

He articulated a new vision of government responsibility, proclaiming that social welfare for its citizens was not just a role for private charities but of government itself in a crisis, "The actual present conditions of life which face at least over two million of the citizens of our state compel a reiteration of the principle to which we are committed, that the people of the state of New York cannot allow any individuals within her borders to go unfed, unclothed, and unsheltered. From that fundamental springs all of the work of relief now in progress in the state."

He was in tune with the sentiments of many when he said those with power and wealth had created the economic collapse and he was determined to act, "The bubble has burst with all its rainbow glory. The public has burned its fingers in the flame of wild speculation and has learned now to fear the fire. While it still fears the fire is the time for us to act."

He noted how the country was in the midst of a great crisis that required a wartime footing. He said the country faced a crisis unlike any since the Civil War:

"I come before you at a time of domestic crisis which calls for the complete laying aside of partisanship and for a unity of leadership and action as complete as if we were engaged in war. Not since the dark days of the Sixties (1860s) have the people of the state and of this nation faced problems as grave, situations as difficult, suffering as severe the economies of America and indeed of the whole world are out of joint. Only the most skillful and concerted care will mend them. That is why I come before you as the governor of all the citizens of the state to ask you to cooperate and counsel with me, not in your capacities as representatives of individual assembly or senatorial districts but rather as a great legislative body acting and speaking for all parts of the state, united in seeking not local advantages but rather the most courageous and hopeful solution of our common problems."

He also acknowledged that the social and political turmoil caused by the Depression had led some to question capitalism and democracy itself,

"increasing concentration of wealth and of the power that wealth controls did not guarantee an intelligent or a fair use of that wealth or power. Today we recognize the unsoundness and the danger."

However, he shared his faith in the American way, "In the many groups of human beings known as nations the structure of government has been so inelastic that reconstruction has been possible only by revolution. We are fortunate that our fathers provided systems, both state and federal, which permit peaceful change by intelligent and representative leadership to meet changing conditions of human society."

Roosevelt took pride about New York State's finances and congratulated legislators and the people of the state, "on the fact that the credit of the state of New York is higher than that of any other unit of government whether it be national, state or local in the whole world."

He was sensitive to the perception that state property taxes were too high but he insisted they had nothing to do with state government since they were local taxes. He cited how many local governments were living beyond their budgets.

He pushed again for fair re-districting with a new census from 1930 at a time when legislative districts could be of any population size that legislators passed in a re-apportionment bill. However, New York failed to agree on a re-apportionment of state Congressional districts after the 1930 census which showed the state gained two additional Congressional seats in the House of Representatives with its growing population. Since there was no agreement on re-districting the two seats were at large statewide seats for the next ten years.

Roosevelt also noted how too many people were living in cities and had left the farmland and proposed that somehow this should be re-balanced. "We seem to have established that the distribution of population during recent years has got out of balance, and that there is a definite overpopulation of the larger communities in the sense that there are too many people in them to maintain a decent living for all. Great problems of distribution of the necessities of life are involved but we have sufficient studies to know that an immediate gain can occur if there are as many people as possible can return closer to the sources of agricultural food supply."

He wanted to re-balance the population and proposed a three-pronged policy to address rural New York that included regional land review and planning to identify how land could be used for industrial production as well as forestry, hunting and recreation. Following the Governor's address, legislators approved key economic measures to allow local governments to spread their budget deficits over a five year period through bond issues.

During that winter, Eleanor Roosevelt spoke in New York to women's groups for 28 states repeating the economic crisis was similar to wartime and urging them to help address the Depression. "The women together can do a great deal. Therefore, let us realize that it is not just for pleasure that we have met and let us try to unite at a time quite as serious as war days," she said.

## The 1932 Lake Placid Olympics

In February, Governor Roosevelt was able to make an impression on the world stage. He had the honor of opening the third Winter Olympic Games which were the first winter games held in the United States at the Adirondack village of Lake Placid. Such an honor would have been available for President Hoover but he chose not to preside. The first winter Olympics had been held in Chamonix, France in 1924 and four years later in St. Moritz, Switzerland. Godfrey Dewey whose family owned the Lake Placid Club attended the games at St. Moritz and came home convinced that Lake Placid could make a bid to host the games. In 1929, Lake Placid was awarded the Olympic games by the International Olympic Committee (IOC).

Just a month after Governor Roosevelt's 1929 visit to Lake Placid the stock market crashed and the Great Depression began. Within months the unemployment rates were rising quickly across the country and the North Country and the Adirondacks. With the Depression causing financial problems for the state Roosevelt threatened to veto a bill that would pay $350,000 for the new Olympic ice arena. He thought that was too much for a facility that was going to be used for a couple weeks for the Olympics and then would just benefit the locals. He settled on $150,000 in a deficiency budget to cover Olympic costs.

Plans were made for building the nation's first bobsled run for the Olympics. In the 1890s the New York State Legislature had protected the Adirondacks from development with "forever wild" designation in the law. This clause prevented the construction of a ski jump on state land. Godfrey Dewey decided that he could solve the problem by donating a plot of land on the Lake Placid Club property to be the site for the bobsled run. This decision would solve the issue but Jewish leaders objected to using state dollars to benefit a private club that discriminated against Jews. Discrimination by private clubs was not politically "incorrect" in those days.

Leaders of the Jewish community pushed their concern and they threatened legal action. They wrote a letter to Governor Roosevelt asking him to intervene but Godfrey Dewey rejected their charges saying the Olympics and the Lake Placid Club were separate, "The fact that the Lake Placid Club does not permit Jews in its membership has no more bearing on the games than the fact the Harvard Club does not admit Yale men; the fact that I am president of the games committee has no bearing on the games." The story became a major issue that was reported in the *New York Times.* In the end, Jewish leaders forced the resolution that the property on which the bobsled was constructed would be given to the state.

In February 1932, 252 athletes from 17 nations came to Lake Placid. The team from Italy, many of whom had never been outside the mountainous regions of their home country, came to New York and marveled at its energy and sites such as the new Empire State Building.

Roosevelt had celebrated his 50th birthday just the week before and he arrived by a special train early that morning. He and Eleanor attended a dinner that evening with 96 people including the top Olympic officials at the Lake Placid Club. On the morning of the games Roosevelt was escorted to the honorary box where he sat along with Godfrey Dewey, Avery Brundage, the head of the United States Olympic Committee and many other officials. Eleanor Roosevelt, Mrs. Dewey, and Mrs. Brundage also sat with them. Mayor Jimmy Walker of New York attended the games and watched the bobsled, the ski jump and other races and kept a busy social schedule.

The parade or "March Past" of the 17 participating nations began with each dipping their flag as they passed Governor Roosevelt. Godfrey Dewey introduced his Excellency Governor Roosevelt who was supposed to just recite the official words opening the games. Instead, Roosevelt abandoned the protocol and made a plea for world peace as Japan had invaded China and fighting raged around Shanghai throughout the games.

"I wish in these latter days that the Olympic ideals of 2800 years ago could have been carried out in one further part. In those days it was the custom every four years, no matter what war was in progress, to cease all obligations of armies during the period of the games. Can those early Olympic ideals be revived throughout all the world so that we can contribute in a larger measure?"

Following the opening ceremonies, in one of the first competitions, Jack Shea skated in front of Roosevelt and won the first of his two gold medals. Shea recalled first meeting Roosevelt in 1929 when Roosevelt said he might see him at the Olympics, "That's one thing that sticks out in my mind because when I crossed the line first I turned and waved to him in the stands. It was like history coming true." That first night of the Olympics the Governor and Eleanor made their way to the Shea home to congratulate Jack on his victories.

As First Lady of New York Mrs. Roosevelt had made several trips to Lake Placid. The *Reading Eagle* reported that "Mrs. Roosevelt was a heroine herself in the eyes of some villagers. She insisted on taking a ride with Harry Homberger, one of the American bobbers. Homberger took her down from zigzag curve to the finish line in a two-man bobber. The bobsled run was the only one of its kind in North America and it was dangerous. The day before the six man German team was seriously injured in an accident."

# PHOTO GALLERY

*Franklin and Eleanor with their five children and Franklin's mother, Sara Delano Roosevelt, Washington, DC 1919*

*Franklin Roosevelt in his first campaign for State Senator,*
*Dutchess County, 1910*

*Franklin Roosevelt re-emerges in public life speaking at 1924*
*Democratic Convention at Madison Square Garden*

*Eleanor and Governor Franklin Roosevelt at his inauguration as Governor, January 1, 1929*

*Governor Roosevelt meeting speedskater Jack Shea, Lake Placid, September 1929* (PHOTO COURTESY OF THE LAKE PLACID OLYMPIC MUSEUM)

*Governor Roosevelt with former Governor Al Smith, 1930*

*Governor Roosevelt presenting an award to his friend,
Admiral Richard Byrd at the Capitol in Albany after
his exploration of the South Pole, June 24, 1930*

*Franklin D. Roosevelt taking the oath of office for his second term with Eleanor and Lt. Governor and Mrs. Herbert Lehman and the Governor's mother Sara Delano Roosevelt behind Eleanor, December 31, 1930*

*Entering the inaugural ball after his second inauguration as Governor, Eleanor Roosevelt, daughter Anna Roosevelt, Governor Roosevelt and Curtis Dall, husband of Anna, January 1, 1931* (THIS IS THE COVER PHOTO)

*Governor Franklin D. Roosevelt at his desk in Albany, January 1, 1931*

*Franklin and Eleanor standing on train platform heading back to Albany during Presidential campaign,1932*

*Governor Roosevelt listening to the radio in the*
*Executive Mansion, Albany, July 1, 1932*

*President Roosevelt signing the Social Security with Frances Perkins*
*behind him, August 14, 1935*

*Eleanor Roosevelt visiting a Works Progress Administration nursery school for African-American children, Des Moines, Iowa, June 1936*

*Eleanor Roosevelt with Queen Elizabeth, June 1939, Hyde Park*

*Franklin and Eleanor with King George VI and Queen Elizabeth, June 1939, Hyde Park*

*Franklin and Eleanor with thirteen grandchildren on the day of his fourth inauguration, January 20, 1945*

*Eleanor Roosevelt in Paris for the United Nations for the
Third General Assembly session, September 1948*

*Eleanor Roosevelt with President Kennedy discussing
Peace Corps, March 1961*

*Eleanor Roosevelt receiving the Mary McLeod Bethune Human Rights Award from Dorothy Height, President of the National Council of Negro Women, 1960*

# CHAPTER 5

## *The Presidential Campaign of 1932*

WHEN 1932 DAWNED FRANKLIN ROOSEVELT was ready to run for President. Roosevelt viewed his activist progressive agenda as a vivid contrast to President Herbert Hoover who believed that the economy would right itself from the Great Depression with little government intervention. On January 23, 1932, Roosevelt announced his candidacy for the Presidency. Roosevelt was well known in the South having spent considerable time at Warm Springs. He had a devoted following in Georgia and on February 12 he authorized his name to be placed on the ballot for the March 23 Georgia primary to elect delegates to the state convention who would elect delegates to the national convention. Major John Cohen, the Democratic national committeeman from Georgia told the *New York Times,* "Your Georgia friends and neighbors feel that you cannot do less than this, a state which is half yours by adoption and wholly yours in esteem and affection of its people." Roosevelt responded, "I do not need to assure you or the people of Georgia of my deep personal affection for what I consider 'my other state'."

Roosevelt won every county in Georgia in the primary and his overall total was 51,498 to 5,541 for a local judge running as a proxy for House Speaker John Nance Garner. In Meriwether County the four precincts which included Warm Springs, Roosevelt won 718-2. In the precinct in Cobb County where the Theodore Roosevelt family had its origins, he won 115-0.

On April 7, Roosevelt gave a key national radio speech in his campaign in which he talked about "the forgotten man" trying to make it economically in those hard times. The speech further earned him national attention and praise as his campaign continued.

Roosevelt was hoping for a first ballot nomination in Chicago. His two main opponents were the Speaker of the House, John Nance Garner of Texas, and his former political ally Al Smith. Smith wanted to win the nomination as he watched Hoover's political support tumble with the high number of unemployed persons after the Depression began. He was also still upset at the bigotry from his 1928 run and he felt he should be given a second chance to defeat the weakened Hoover. He viewed Roosevelt as his protege whom he had elevated to the governorship and now was in a prime position to win the nomination and Presidency.

Roosevelt won most of the primaries held in the spring and had the largest number of delegates awarded. However, nominations were not won in the primaries in those days. Party leaders still controlled most of the delegates. Two thirds of the delegates were needed to clinch the nomination and Roosevelt had over 50% but not two thirds. Roosevelt was staking out the progressive ground of the party which still was dominated by centrists and conservatives.

However, in late April Smith won thirty six delegates in the Massachusetts primary and another fourteen in Pennsylvania. The anti-Roosevelt forces figured they would have over 400 delegates which would be enough to deny Roosevelt a first ballot victory.

When he arrived in Georgia on April 30 for his spring visit there Roosevelt was met at the Warm Springs train station by patients and local party leaders. His state campaign manager W.E. Pate boarded

## A gift for you

This book was written by my boss at the NYS Office for the Aging. Hope you enjoy it. From Gail Koser

the train in Charlotte, North Carolina to travel with the Governor to Atlanta. He told him that Al Smith would lose the South again if he were nominated and that even his supporters from 1928 were annoyed that he was threatening the party harmony. Southerners again viewed Al Smith as part of the urban, immigrant population of northern cities, run by political machines.

Roosevelt's health was always an issue that his political opponents sought to question. He was very careful to make sure that he was not photographed getting in and out of a car and the media still generally complied and did not try to show photos of his struggle to get to his feet. The public did see him often holding the shoulder of one of his sons who appeared at political events with him during his time as Governor.

The previous year, on July 25, 1931, *Liberty* magazine published an article by journalist Earle Locker, "Is Franklin Roosevelt physically fit to be President?" Roosevelt agreed to submit to a thorough medical examination by a number of doctors. They concluded that Roosevelt's "health and powers of endurance are such as to allow him to meet any demands of private and public life." The author also concluded "that he seems able to take more punishment than many men ten years younger." Anyone who saw him knew he had stamina as he had shown in his vigorous campaigns and travels around the state." The article helped to quiet the questions and doubts expressed.

Eleanor's perspective was that Franklin's polio played a major role in enhancing his political prospects, "Franklin's illness was another turning point, and proved a blessing in disguise; for it gave him strength and courage he had not had before. He had to think out the fundamentals of living and learn the greatest of all lessons - infinite patience and never-ending persistence." Many Americans saw him sympathetically and even heroically as having succeeded in living an active life despite having a major physical disability.

Other friends and supporters were visiting Roosevelt in Georgia. One from Missouri told him of a "whispering plot" of misinformation that his health condition was very serious and that he came to Warm Springs on a stretcher. It was suggested that he was not capable of serving as President. Urged to respond by engaging in some physical activity to show his strength, Roosevelt responded that he didn't need to respond because the public could see how active he had been as Governor of New York and that people could see he was in better shape than any time since he got polio.

Also visiting Roosevelt in Warm Springs in May was his state Conservation Commissioner and close friend Henry Morgenthau Jr who had just visited a number of farm states in the Midwest. He said the support for Roosevelt among farmers there was strong and that many were aware of the agricultural support programs he had established in New York.

President Hoover's political troubles mounted further in the spring of 1932 as a "Bonus Army" of World War I veterans descended on Washington and built an encampment to protest for economic relief and petition for the immediate awarding of future bonuses promised. Hoover got fed up with their presence and called on Army General Douglas MacArthur to rout the protestors including their wives and children and burn their encampment shelter and belongings, a response that was widely condemned.

## The Democratic Convention

When the Democratic convention began in New York in July Al Smith was hoping to stop Roosevelt and after several ballots have the delegates swing toward him. Roosevelt had the lead after the first three convention ballots and Smith and Garner, along with two other previous Democratic nominees, John W. Davis and James Cox, were all hoping to prolong the contest and have it swing in their direction.

The Roosevelt forces were very concerned that the longer the balloting went on, his support might peak and then collapse, allowing someone else to win the nomination. That scenario remained a concern after Roosevelt only gained a few additional votes on the second and third ballots. Friday was a tense day as the family listened to the balloting on the radio from Albany. Press tables had been set up in the garage behind the mansion and Eleanor kept them supplied with tea and coffee.

Roosevelt reached out to William McAdoo and the California delegation which with Texas was supporting Garner. McAdoo still remembered his deadlock at the 1924 convention with Al Smith and he agreed to a deal to support Roosevelt. Then, Texas agreed to support Roosevelt if Garner was selected as the Vice Presidential candidate. Roosevelt chose Garner to secure the ballots needed. So with Texas and California Roosevelt won on the fourth ballot. Al Smith refused to make the vote unanimous but eventually he would campaign and support Roosevelt. President Hoover felt that Roosevelt would be the easiest of the candidates to defeat given his physical condition. He viewed Roosevelt as a political lightweight.

Roosevelt left Albany on Saturday morning and took off for Chicago to address the convention, becoming the first nominee to do so. Usually, the nominee would wait until he had been officially informed of his victory and then a formal acceptance would come later. Roosevelt had decided to break the precedent though and fly to Chicago. Though Roosevelt didn't like flying he chartered a private plane from Albany airport and his party made their way in stiff headwinds and had to stop twice in Buffalo and Cleveland. His son Elliott wrote in a biography of his father, "Weeks earlier, he decided to fly so that he could deliver his acceptance speech in person, not dawdle across the country by train...He also wanted to demonstrate by this gesture that he was a man of vigorous action, not the semi-invalid depicted without fail by his enemies in both parties. Above all, he knew that by smashing precedent by accepting on the spot, he could thrill the voters with a sense of decisive leadership and get his campaign off to an instant start."

Elliott and his brother James joined him for the flight along with Missy LeHand and Eleanor, Gus Gennerich and Earl Miller who were personal assistants. Friends and neighbors saw them off from the mansion. The plane arrived in Chicago two hours late but Roosevelt was mobbed at the airport by thousands of people who got so close to him his hat went flying and his glasses were dislodged. Chicago Mayor Anton Cermak also greeted him at the airport.

In his acceptance speech, Roosevelt uttered words that became famous, "I pledge you, I pledge myself to a new deal for the American people. Let us all here assembled constitute ourselves prophets of a new order of competence and of courage. This is more than a political campaign; it is a call to arms. Give me your help, not to win votes alone, but to win in this crusade to restore America to its own people."

Roosevelt had chosen "Anchors Aweigh" for his campaign song, but Louis Howe couldn't stand the song so Roosevelt wanted the convention band to play "Happy Days are Here Again."

Roosevelt returned to Albany after the convention and on July 6th 15,000 people took part in a homecoming torch parade celebration through the streets of Albany to the Executive Mansion with eleven bands playing. The Albany County Democratic machine put out orders to fill the streets near the mansion. Albany Mayor John Boyd Thacher welcomed Governor Roosevelt back to Albany and pledged to turn out the largest plurality in history for a presidential candidate in the Albany area. The Governor and Presidential nominee then addressed what the *New York Times* described as a "tightly packed audience that thronged the lawn of the Executive Mansion and spread into neighboring streets." He mentioned his long association with Albany going back to the turn of the century when he attended the inauguration "of a certain cousin of mine." Roosevelt also pledged that he would support the party's platform to end Prohibition though he would defer to Congress to lead that effort for repeal.

More homecoming celebrations were held with his friends in Hyde Park.

Roosevelt was about to set off on a vacation sail with his sons through the Cape Cod Canal. He was ready after that to begin his nationwide campaign. He could not make his usual summer inspection tour around New York State and he asked Lt. Governor Herbert Lehman to take his place, an overt endorsement of Lehman's bid for the gubernatorial nomination now that Roosevelt was running for President.

Lehman would win the nomination for Governor but only after Tammany Hall had tried to defeat him. It had built an alliance with the O'Connell brothers who led the party in Albany and their first choice was Albany Mayor Thacher. If not Thacher, they wanted to have Senator Robert Wagner run for Governor and Lehman for his Senate seat. Lehman said he would only seek the Governor's seat and Al Smith and Roosevelt stood with him against Tammany and he won the nomination.

## Mayor Jimmy Walker and the Balancing Act

As Roosevelt was preparing to campaign across the country for the White House in the summer of 1932, he was confronted again by Tammany corruption in New York City and what to do with Jimmy Walker, the flamboyant Mayor of New York City, who was facing calls for his removal. Only the Governor could remove a Mayor for incompetence or unethical activities. Running for President, Roosevelt was the focus of great political attention and was under pressure to take action against Walker's corruption.

Walker had been around politics as long as Roosevelt and Al Smith serving in the state Assembly from 1910-1915. He was then elected to the State Senate and in 1925 he was elected Mayor of New York with the backing of Governor Smith. In 1929 he was re-elected, defeating Republican Fiorello LaGuardia. Walker was a flamboyant, debonair Mayor who some compared to a movie star or celebrity during the Jazz Age era when Prohibition was openly flouted in speakeasies in the city and elsewhere. He was so popular and reports of corruption were so common that many tolerated it.

During his tenure though, a major scandal erupted about bribery in the New York City court and parole system, exposing how police had targeted women without the legal ability to defend themselves and forced them to pay thousands of dollars to be cleared. Walker was also charged with using city contracts to financially benefit his friends and receiving gifts from persons seeking city public transit business.

The State Legislature with its Republican majorities in both houses had approved an investigation committee to be headed by respected, retired Judge John Seabury whose name became attached to the commission. After public hearings were held with the Mayor, Seabury sent a letter to Governor Roosevelt saying, "the Mayor's conduct has been characterized by such malfeasance and nonfeasance in disregard of the duties of his office as Mayor and he has conducted himself, to the prejudice of the City of New York and its inhabitants, in a manner so far unbecoming the high office which he holds as to render him unfit to continue in the office of Mayor."

The decision in the case would be a tricky balancing act for Roosevelt because he needed Tammany's enthusiastic support in his presidential campaign, but he needed to show voters nationwide that he was an independent, fair-minded politician. He did not want to be viewed as under the influence of machine politics as some voters had viewed Al Smith in 1928. Republicans had been trying to make the excesses of Tammany Hall a campaign issue but Roosevelt had always been wily in his dealings with the party bosses and never under their control.

Roosevelt waited for the report of the Seabury commission and then used it to hold hearings with Walker for three weeks beginning on August 11, while holding off on his Presidential campaign. In the hearing he publicly questioned Walker about having presided over the corruption and peppered him with questions about his finances and where he got all his money. Walker disagreed with the charges being hurled at him and felt he was the victim of a "hoax."

Years later Roosevelt told a story about Walker during the trial, "Jimmy Walker, once upon a time, was living openly with this gal all over New York, including the house across the street from me. She was an extremely attractive little tart. Jimmy and his wife had separated for all intents and purposes. And it came to my trial before me was Jimmy Walker, 1932 and Jimmy goes and hires his former wife, for $10,000, to come up to Albany on a Saturday. Jimmy was a good Catholic and he hadn't been to church in five whole years and he paid his wife $10,000 to go up there to Albany on a Friday afternoon after my trial had finished for the week and we were to go on (again) on Monday. Jimmy had never spent a Sunday in Albany in his life but Mrs. Walker comes up to Albany, lives with him extensively in the same suite in the hotel and on Sunday the two of them go to mass at the Albany cathedral together. Price? $10,000."

With the intense publicity of Roosevelt's hearings, Walker was told by Al Smith who had been his long-time supporter, that he couldn't survive as Mayor. Finally, during a break for Labor Day on September 1, 1932, Walker resigned under pressure. Roosevelt had proven his independence from Tammany Hall while he stood for honest government not controlled by political bosses.

An interim Mayor was appointed and a split in the Democratic Party in 1933 led to the election of the progressive Republican Fiorello LaGuardia.


## The Campaign

With the Walker hearings over, Roosevelt began his characteristic vigorous campaigning across the country. He presented an image of hope, optimism and action in contrast to Hoover who seemed unable to make headway against the Depression. Roosevelt traveled over 9000 miles in less than a month in the fall and then returned to Albany and made trips from there to New England and other states. He met with over 20,000 farmers in Topeka, Kansas and made 15 other major addresses including many more informal speeches along the railroad tracks where hundreds turned out. He called them his "my little boy Jimmy" speeches because his son was riding with him.

Roosevelt made his last speech at a rally in Poughkeepsie the night before the election. He spent that night alone in Hyde Park while the rest of the family was in New York.

Hoover's failure to effectively deal with the economic carnage of the Depression set the stage for an historic landslide on election night as Roosevelt won all states except Pennsylvania and four small ones in New England: Vermont, New Hampshire, Maine and Connecticut.

Though President Hoover was not greatly impressed with Roosevelt's abilities, he sent a cordial message of congratulations, "I wish for you a most successful administration. In the common purpose of all of us I shall dedicate myself to every possible helpful effort." Roosevelt responded, "I appreciate your generous telegram. For the immediate as well as for the most distant future I join in your gracious expression of a common purpose in helpful effort for our country."

Roosevelt also stressed that he would still need to attend to his duties as Governor of New York until January 1st and then he would be out of office for two months. In those days, the presidential in-auguration was not held until March, four months after the election. Roosevelt's inauguration would be the last to be held in March. (The twentieth amendment enacted on January 23, 1933 changed the date to January 20 beginning in 1937).

Roosevelt and Hoover met at the White House in November and focused on the financial crisis. Hoover attempted to get Roosevelt to sign on to some of his initiatives in the time after the election but Roosevelt was not interested in being drawn into resolving issues since he was not in charge of the country. He would not be making any decisions regarding Cabinet positions for two months.

Eleanor Roosevelt had not been thrilled with Franklin's desire to be President but she knew for a long time that winning the White House was his political goal: "From the personal standpoint, I did not want my husband to be president. I realized however that it was impossible to keep a man out of public service when that was what he wanted and was undoubtedly well-equipped for. It was pure selfish-ness on my part and I never mentioned my feelings on the subject to him. I did not work directly in the campaign because I felt that was something better done by others but I went on many of the trips and always did anything that Franklin felt would be helpful."

In a December interview for a feature about her working life as a teacher, Eleanor was asked about how some questioned about wom-en working and taking jobs from married men heading households during the Depression.

"The principle of denying work to anyone who wants to work, married, or single, is an obnoxious one. It is a dangerous and terrible thing to do. Frequently, a married woman has parents or other dependents whom she must support or she must supplement her husband's income to give her children the opportunities they need. Moreover, no one can judge the subjective value and necessity of work for another person. If, during this emergency a married woman voluntarily relinquishes her job to another, it may be a very fine thing for her to do. But her job should not be withheld from her on account of her status."

A few weeks after the election, Roosevelt's fourth grandchild was born in New York City at the Harbor Sanitarium. Eleanor had given the mansion telephone operator in Albany a message to put through a long distance call when news came. She got the call shortly after 2:00 am on November 17th and she got dressed and headed for Union Station to take the train to New York. She realized she didn't have any money so she had to ask a Secret Service agent assigned to the President-elect for $10 to cover the taxi and train fare. She arrived at the hospital at 6:30 am, an hour after the baby was born. She tried to call the mansion at 8:00 am but the butler wouldn't accept the call because he didn't think she had even left the mansion.

The President-elect spent his last day as Governor, on New Year's Eve cleaning out his desk at the Executive Mansion in Albany. In the evening the Roosevelts held a special meal for Cabinet officials. Many were not in attendance because of an epidemic of the flu. Later they went to the inaugural ball at the Armory and then went back to the Governor's mansion to say goodbye to the staff that had served them. They left for a car ride to Hyde Park at 11:10 pm, with four Secret Service agents in a car behind them. Bells and whistles greeted them in Hudson at midnight to signal the new year and they arrived at Hyde Park at 1:00 am. They would return to Albany on January 2 for the public inauguration of Governor Lehman.

Roosevelt spent the first weeks of January meeting with some members of Congress in Hyde Park before going to Warm Springs for more relaxation and therapy. Later in January, FDR went to Florida for a vacation and a fishing cruise. Returning to Miami, he got out of his car to make a speech when Giuseppe Zangara, an immigrant from Italy's Calabria province, fired shots at him, missing the President-elect but hitting five others including Roosevelt's friend, Mayor Anton Cermak of Chicago. Roosevelt held Cermak up as the car sped to the hospital and was totally calm and kept speaking to the Mayor saying he would be okay. Roosevelt's aides remarked later that they were amazed at how calm he was in dealing with the shooting.

Eleanor was in New York and she was told about the shooting when she arrived back at the home. Soon she got a call from her husband. She told others he was all right and then she departed for Grand Central Station and a trip to Ithaca for a speech the next day. Roosevelt visited the victims in the following days. Cermak died nineteen days later. Zangara pleaded guilty and was sentenced to death in the electric chair. Before the switch was pulled, he said, ""Viva l'Italia! Goodbye to all poor peoples everywhere!"

A week after the shooting a bomb was sent in the mail addressed to Roosevelt from Watertown, New York. It was traced to another Calabrian, 21 year old Joseph Doldo of Watertown. He sent more bombs and he went to prison for sixteen years.

Before heading to Washington for his inauguration, Roosevelt and Al Smith had a friendly evening in Albany again, attending the annual Legislative Correspondents Association dinner. Like the Gridiron dinner in Washington the Correspondents show is a night for satire and humor aimed at public officials in New York State. The theme of the night during Prohibition was "Foam Sweet Foam" and depicted a saloon that had a sign that said, "Closed Since 1921 by Andrew Volstead." Uncle Sam, pictured as Roosevelt, breaks the padlock and finds the bartender is Al Smith. The entire cast sang, "Franklin Can you Spare a Job?"

# CHAPTER 6

## Albany Comes to Washington:
## President Roosevelt and the New Deal

ON MARCH 4, 1933, Franklin Roosevelt took the oath of office from Chief Justice Charles Evans Hughes with his hand on the same 1686 Dutch language family Bible he had used in Albany when he was sworn in as Governor in 1929 and 1931. Roosevelt had first gone to the White House to meet President Hoover but the admiration and friendship of years earlier had turned into a frosty relationship. They barely spoke on the ride to the Capitol inauguration from the White House.

Roosevelt was immediately confronting the dire economic situation created by the Great Depression. He faced a banking crisis that threatened the financial system. Banks were failing and closing. 4004 banks with $3.6 billion in deposits failed in the first two months of 1933. Roosevelt called for a four day national bank "holiday," that closed banks. Many states had already done so. New York, Illinois and Pennsylvania had ordered banks in their states closed on the morning of the inaugural. 12 million people, more than 25% of the workforce were unemployed.

Capitalism itself was on trial with many angry at Wall Street speculators who had brought on the Depression. Farmers were so angry they broke up bankruptcy auctions. Thousands had occupied the Nebraska statehouse. There were fears of a violent revolution. So, Roosevelt's desire for action was well received.

Dictators were rising in the Soviet Union, Italy and Germany. Mussolini had been admired for "getting the trains running on time," and the same week as FDR took power, Adolf Hitler was grabbing and consolidating more power in Germany. There was a sentiment among some for a leader to use wartime powers or even assume the role of a benign dictator if he could fix the crisis. They were not looking for a police state but to provide a leader with emergency powers to take executive actions. In his inaugural address Roosevelt himself made reference to the possible need for such powers and it was that statement which got the loudest applause and drew much attention the next day,

"I am prepared under my constitutional duty to recommend the measures that a stricken nation in the midst of a stricken world may require. These measures, or such other measures as the Congress may build out of its experience and wisdom, I shall seek, within my constitutional authority, to bring to speedy adoption. But in the event that the Congress shall fail to take one of these two courses, and in the event that the national emergency is still critical, I shall not evade the clear course of duty that will then confront me. I shall ask the Congress for the one remaining instrument to meet the crisis — broad Executive power to wage a war against the emergency, as great as the power that would be given to me if we were in fact invaded by a foreign foe."

FDR's own confidence in government action to deal with the economic crisis inspired the country. His voice rang out with a talk about fear that would later become his most famous phrase in that address:

"So, first of all, let me assert my firm belief that the only thing we have to fear is fear itself--nameless, unreasoning, unjustified terror which paralyzes needed efforts to convert retreat into advance. In every dark hour of our national life a leadership of frankness and vigor has met with that understanding and support of the people themselves which is essential to victory. I am convinced that you will again give that support to leadership in these critical days.

He took aim at those who had caused the Depression, using Biblical references:

"the rulers of the exchange of mankind's goods have failed, through their own stubbornness and their own incompetence, have admitted their failure, and abdicated. Practices of the unscrupulous money changers stand indicted in the court of public opinion, rejected by the hearts and minds of men. The money changers have fled from their high seats in the temple of our civilization. We may now restore that temple to the ancient truths. The measure of the restoration lies in the extent to which we apply social values more noble than mere monetary profit."

Then, he gave some almost religious advice that echoes some of his speeches as Governor, that the pursuit of riches was not the highest goal of life.

"Happiness lies not in the mere possession of money, it lies in the joy of achievement, in the thrill of creative effort. The joy and moral stimulation of work no longer must be forgotten in the mad chase of evanescent profits. These dark days will be worth all they cost us if they teach us that our true destiny is not to be ministered unto but to minister to ourselves and to our fellow men."

He concluded by expressing his faith in democracy,

"We do not distrust the future of essential democracy. The people of the United States have not failed. In their need they have registered a mandate that they want direct, vigorous action. They have asked for discipline and direction under leadership. They have made me the present instrument of their wishes. In the spirit of the gift I take it. In this dedication of a Nation we humbly ask the blessing of God. May He protect each and every one of us. May He guide me in the days to come."

Indeed, as Frances Perkins noted, his way of throwing his head around that had seemed so arrogant when he was a young state Senator now seemed so self-assured. As Jonathan Alter wrote in *The Defining Moment:*

"That March of 1933, the new president did not have to mobilize aging members of the American legion under martial law. Franklin Roosevelt mobilized himself and his latent talent for leadership. He found his voice and his voice defined America."

The policies he promoted and enacted with the Legislature in New York as Governor were a blueprint for some of the policies and programs he would pursue in Washington, particularly unemployment insurance, work relief programs, public water power, and Social Security. Eleanor Roosevelt recounted in her autobiography, "The work in Albany was, of course, invaluable in background for the work that was to come. There he had the experience of working with legislative groups in which his political party was in the minority. The years in Albany cast their shadow before them."

Roosevelt was determined to move quickly and his first one hundred days became an historic period of social and economic legislation to restore faith in the American economy. He brought with him from Albany several key members of his Albany administration to form a "Brain Trust." Ray Moley, Louis Howe, and Samuel Rosenman were key political advisors. He brought agency heads from Albany, Frances Perkins, Henry Morgenthau and Harry Hopkins, to design and lead the programs that became the New Deal.

He immediately began using the radio to reach the people. Just eight days after his inauguration on Sunday night, March 12, he broadcast his first fireside chat as President and his confident, friendly and relatable manner began to lift the spirits of those listening, just like they had in New York. Like a teacher he explained the banking system and why the banks were closed for a "bank holiday" due to a panic. saying that "hoarding has become an exceedingly unfashionable past time." He told them banks would re-open and that the public also had a responsibility to have confidence and again make deposits to banks that would be safe. "It is safer to keep your money in a re-opened bank than it is to keep it under your mattress."

In the course of a little over 100 days, Congress passed fifteen major laws that would provide employment and relief, labor protections and banking reform. The Glass-Steagall Act separated investment and consumer banking and it established the Federal Deposit Insurance Corporation (FDIC) to guarantee savings. The Securities and Exchange Commission (SEC) would regulate Wall Street trading.

## Civil Conservation Corps (CCC) and Relief Programs

After he worked with his staff and Congress to develop the Emergency Banking Act to re-open the banks, Roosevelt immediately began addressing the unemployment crisis in the country by sending legislation to Congress establishing a number of programs to put people to work with public dollars.

Roosevelt appointed Harry Hopkins to assume control of employment and public works programs like he had in Albany. These included the Work Progress Administration (WPA), Federal Emergency Relief Administration (FERA), and the Civil Works Administration (CWA) Hopkins became one of Roosevelt's most trusted aides who he later appointed Secretary of Commerce in his second term. Hopkins was such an important advisor that he moved into the White House to live for several years.

Roosevelt hired Harold Ickes of Chicago who became a key Cabinet official as Secretary of the Interior and the director of the Work Progress Administration (WPA) which would provide massive funding for public infrastructure projects such as parks, airports, roads, bridges and housing. It also supported artists to draw posters for national parks, writers and others. From 1935 to 1943, 8.5 million persons had jobs on WPA projects.

FDR later dispatched Hopkins to Britain to be a liaison with Churchill during World War II. FDR even thought of him as a possible successor in 1940 but Hopkins had serious health problems.

Morgenthau, his neighbor and trusted friend who served as Agriculture Commissioner in Albany, was first appointed as Under Secretary of the Treasury but then became the Secretary, giving him the key role in economic recovery policies.

The other key appointment who was both an architect and administrator of the New Deal was Frances Perkins. Roosevelt brought her to Washington to serve as Labor Secretary, the first woman in American history to serve in a President's Cabinet. Perkins tried to talk him out of appointing her. She felt the Secretary had always been someone from the unions and that if he wanted a woman, he should find one who came from the union working world who in her view would be more appropriate in the role. Roosevelt wanted Perkins though because he knew her and had confidence in her.

She told FDR that she would take the job but wanted him to commit to a progressive agenda to further what she and Roosevelt had been doing in New York on labor and social welfare. Her priorities included minimum wage legislation, ending child labor, unemployment insurance and a establishing a forty hour work week instead of forty eight hours common at the time. In many ways, the key programs of the New Deal were her agenda that Roosevelt accepted and committed to act on.

Roosevelt and Democratic Congressional leaders wanted to strengthen the power of labor unions. They moved quickly to pass the National Labor Relations Act (NLRA) or Wagner Act sponsored by New York Senator Robert Wagner. This act gave labor unions the right to organize, the right to collective bargaining, the right to strike and banned company unions.

Soon after Roosevelt was inaugurated, the new Democratic Congress, reflecting a growing public desire to end Prohibition, voted to allow some beverages with a small amount of alcohol to be produced. During 1933, many states held conventions and voted to repeal the 18th amendment that approved Prohibition. Roosevelt had long felt the issue should be left to the states and on December 5, 1933 the 21st amendment went into effect repealing Prohibition after enough states enacted it. Control of alcohol was returned to the states and localities and most allowed alcohol again but many localities remained "dry" for many years.

The Civilian Conservation Corps (CCC) was one of the earliest and most popular work projects of the New Deal that built on the TERA program in New York. Roosevelt loved the idea of sending unemployed men into the countryside to work on projects to protect the environment. He wanted to move quickly to take action to put people to work and the CCC was a priority. He called an emergency session of Congress on March 21. On March 27 Roosevelt introduced the Emergency Conservation Work Act which passed both houses of Congress on March 31. Then, FDR created the agency by Executive order on April 5 and just three days later the first person was enrolled in the program. The program lasted for nine years until manpower needs in World War II became more important.

When the Bonus Army returned to Washington to protest in the spring of 1933, Roosevelt sent Eleanor to visit and socialize with them instead of shooting at them. He signed an executive order allowing 25,000 to quickly join the CCC and waive some of the requirements for them. Nearly 250,000 veterans from the Spanish American War and World War I would eventually participate in the CCC which was credited with a dramatic reduction in crime.

The Army, the Forestry Service and the Department of Labor were on the committee that oversaw the program. The Army had the facilities to house large numbers of men, the Labor Department could select them and the forestry service would determine the projects.

Men from cities and no experience with outdoor work and equipment would have to be physically fit and trained for the jobs. A National Reemployment Service agency was developed in a few days and it would make the rules to recruit 250,000 men who were unemployed. Secretary of the Army George Dern was pleased to work with the program and felt it was a very important experience. Frances Perkins noted that at a Cabinet meeting Dern had said, "They have had to learn to govern men by leadership, explanation and diplomacy rather than discipline. The knowledge is priceless to the American Army."

The CCC provided shelter, food and clothing and a $30 monthly stipend to workers. At its peak in August 1935 there were nearly 506,000 enrolled at 2900 camps across the nation. Through the life of the program, three million young men participated. The program provided education, training and a sense of purpose to young men ages 17-28 who were unemployed. They were able to perform many projects in ten categories:

1. **Structural improvements:** bridges, fire lookout towers, service buildings
2. **Transportation:** truck trails, minor roads, foot trails and airport landing fields

3. **Erosion control:** check dams, terracing, and vegetable covering

4. **Flood control**: irrigation, drainage, dams, ditching, channel work

5. **Forest culture:** planting trees and shrubs, timber stand improvement, seed collection, nursery work

6. **Forest protection:** fire prevention, fire pre-suppression, firefighting, insect and disease control

7. **Landscape and recreation:** public camp and picnic ground development, lake and pond site clearing and development

8. **Range:** elimination of predatory animals

9. **Wildlife:** stream improvement, fish stocking, food and cover planting

10. **Emergency work:** surveys, mosquito control

In New York State, there were over 200 camps. CCC workers built golf courses, roads and cabins at many state parks. A company of Spanish American war veterans built cabins, trails, a golf course and clubhouse at the Green Lakes State Park in Central New York. Others worked at Bear Mountain State Park, Fair Haven State Park and Gilbert State Park and Allegany State Park. The CCC camp in Delmar outside of Albany was built by Company 270 as an experimental game farm and today is the Five Rivers Environmental Education Center. At the time of the 50th reunion of the CCC Alexander Woehrle of the Albany area remarked in 1990, "For those of us out of New York City, we traveled to rural parts of the country we had never known and probably would never have seen otherwise."

Some of the camps were closed during World War II and used as prisoner of war camps.

## Social Security, Unemployment Insurance and Aid to Families and Children

The economic plight of older persons during the Great Depression when many lost their jobs and had no other source of income accelerated a movement for a national pension plan during FDR's first term in the White House. European countries had enacted social insurance and old age pensions decades earlier. In 1912, Theodore Roosevelt had run on a Progressive Party platform that included old age pensions. Dr. Francis Townsend had written a letter to the editor in California outlining a simple pension plan that promised $200 per month to retirees with a 2% national tax to support it. Townsend wanted this pension available to persons age 60 and older not just to provide financial security for them, but to entice many to retire. Large scale retirements would create new job openings for desperate, unemployed, younger persons during the Depression. The plan was considered to be unrealistic given that the average working person earned only $100 per month in the 1930s.

Even so, Townsend's plan became so popular that as many as 5000 local Townsend Clubs were formed across the country to advocate for it. Seventeen states had enacted old age pension programs with New York, California and Massachusetts providing 87% of all benefits in the country.

The grassroots advocacy for the Townsend Plan played an important role in the drive to get the Social Security bill passed in 1935. President Roosevelt and Frances Perkins believed that passing a Social Security Act in 1935 was critical because they feared the political pressure building for the Townsend Plan might be unstoppable.

While Roosevelt's proposal for the government to provide a system of social insurance was revolutionary, the Townsend campaign and other proposals went further and were part of a strong populist left wing. Senator Huey Long of Louisiana and Father Charles Coughlin, a Catholic radio priest from Detroit were pushing more radical plans along with California Governor candidate Upton Sinclair who was pushing a Share the Wealth plan. Roosevelt was concerned about a political challenge from the left and he told a reporter in early 1935, "I am fighting Communism, Huey Longism, Coughlinism, Townsendism."

After passing work relief and banking legislation to address the immediate financial crisis when the Roosevelt Administration began in 1933, attention began to focus on other economic legislation which would have a long lasting impact. Many of the New Deal programs were viewed as temporary emergency programs to address the financial crisis. Roosevelt wanted to dramatically project the government's role by providing "cradle to grave" security for Americans against the prospects of any future depression. Perkins was appointed to chair a Committee on Economic Security in 1934 to develop a program that would include an old age pension program, unemployment insurance and programs for families and children. The proposal was also to include a national health insurance program. Hearings were held and legislation was developed. That addition caused the American Medical Association (AMA) representing doctors across the country to mount a vigorous campaign against it, calling it "socialized medicine." FDR and Perkins did not want to risk the fate of the entire bill so they eventually dropped the health insurance plan.

Still, the legislation did not pass without a fight and negotiations. Roosevelt introduced his bill on January 17, 1935. Despite its eventual success there were many roadblocks and compromises. Some in his administration were concerned that the conservative Supreme Court would rule the legislation was unconstitutional as it had other New Deal programs. There was a concern that maybe the program's taxes would take too much money out of the economy and thwart recovery. It was a bill that maintained his insistence that it follow an insurance model with payroll contributions by employees and employers. As he had advocated as Governor, he did not want it viewed as part of the "the dole" or welfare. He did not want it viewed as a right either but as "property" which workers owned with their contributions.

The only direct relief in the bill was $50 million in federal grants for the states for immediate financial support for the poor elderly, already retired and another $25 million for the Aid to Dependent Children program. Some had wanted more direct relief because they considered the payroll tax to be very regressive.

To many, the bill was not perfect and compromises had to be made that didn't seem equitable but they were needed to deal with pragmatic economic realities. The bill excluded 9.4 million poor people who were farm laborers and domestic servants because of its economic impact of contributions on employers with less than ten workers.

The final bill passed the Congress by overwhelming margins. The House passed it first in April 1935 by a vote of 371 to 33. After the Senate passed it 77 to 6 the bill went to a conference committee. It included Social Security, unemployment insurance with cost sharing with the states along with the Aid to Families with Dependent Children (AFDC) program. The unemployment plan included up to sixteen weeks of benefits with up to half pay to a maximum of $15 per week. It included a 1% payroll tax which was also a problem since during the Depression any extra costs taken from paychecks were significant. The final bill was passed in August and was signed by President Roosevelt on August 14, 1935, a date its supporters have marked on major anniversaries.

Roosevelt felt that the Social Security Act was the most important bill of the New Deal and said if nothing else was done in that session of Congress it would be historic. He viewed it as the fulfillment of his vision in New York State that an old age pension program not be a welfare program but a program of insurance with employee contributions.

In his remarks he alluded to his knowledge of the years of advocacy for such a plan,

"Today, a hope of many years standing is in large part fulfilled. The civilization of the past hundred years with startling industrial changes has tended more and more to make life more insecure. ..... This Social Security measure gives at least some protection to 30 million of our citizens who will reap direct benefits through unemployment compensation, through old age pensions and through the increased services for the protection of children services and the prevention of ill health."

"We can never insure 100% of the population against 100% of the hazards or vicissitudes of life but we have tried to frame a law which will give some measure of protection to the average citizen and his family against the loss of a job and against poverty ridden old age."

Within a year, one million persons were enrolled in the program and the first benefits were paid in January 1940 to 76-year old Ida Fuller of Vermont who received $41.30 per month.

In 1939 there were amendments to the act to include the spouses of deceased workers and a reduction in the payroll tax to prevent too large a surplus.

Social Security became the most successful and popular government program. However, the decision to drop health care was a politically fateful one because it would take three decades to win passage of Medicare and Medicaid in 1965. It was 75 years before the Affordable Care Act was passed in 2010 during the Obama Administration to extend health insurance to those who did not have coverage through an employer or private insurance or were not disabled or old enough for Medicare or with an income below Medicaid eligibility levels.

Years later, New York senior citizen activist Rose Kryzak of Queens recalled the campaign for Social Security and the enthusiasm for Roosevelt's plans:

"It got to a point when FDR talked about changes people flocked to him. I went to many rallies. I remember when my father got his first Social Security check. $50 was the minimum that my father got; there was a tremendous celebration in the community. That was the first check that came and people were kissing and hugging each other because they won such a tremendous victory."

Max Manes, a long time senior and union activist recalled how difficult it was to be a hatmaker in the 1930s. Years later he wrote about the struggle for income security,

"I remember when Social Security was enacted and I remember the joy with which it was welcomed. Like workers in other industries we - members of the old United Hatters of North America now called the Amalgamated Clothing and Textile Workers - felt strongly the need for a national system of social insurance and we made ourselves work hard on it. Working in seasonal industry with chronic slack periods and layoffs with no unemployment insurance and no pensions for the aged, we knew what it meant to lose the normal source of income. Those among us who could no longer work ... were subjected to degrading means to prove need, and their children had to prove they were unable to support them before they could qualify for any assistance. A benefit for widows and other survivors which was paid for them from union dues collapsed after the Wall Street crash in 1929 as did similar such plans in other industries. For us the enactment of Social Security was like a dream come true."

## The TVA and Electric Power

Other policies that followed Roosevelt's work in Albany included the creation of the Tennessee Valley Authority (TVA) as a public agency in 1933 to harness hydropower from the Tennessee River, modernize farming in the region and the building of dams for flood control. The TVA helped to bring electricity to rural areas in the Appalachian region and in Mississippi, Alabama, Georgia and the Carolinas and its projects unleashed economic development in poverty stricken areas.

In 1935 Roosevelt signed an executive order to create the Rural Electrification Administration (REA) which would lend money to farm cooperatives to finance electric lines in the rural areas that private companies would not serve. The following year Congress passed legislation to put the agency in law and to provide funding and support for the agency. Only 3% of rural residents had access to electricity in the early 1930s. The REA drove down electricity prices and brought electric lighting, sewing machines and radios to 90 percent of the rural Americans by the late 1950s.

Roosevelt's plan for St. Lawrence River hydropower though was never built during his term as Governor or as President.

## Eleanor Roosevelt as First Lady and Advocate for Social Justice

Eleanor Roosevelt used her position as First Lady to be an advocate with her husband for many social justice causes. She was the President's eyes and ears and went to see the Depression era economic conditions that many people faced. She also wanted to see the impact of New Deal programs. She went to West Virginia to see the plight of miners who had lost their jobs. There is a famed picture of her emerging from a trip down a mineshaft. She saw communities devastated by the Depression in the Appalachian region and she became involved in a New Deal effort that created a new community called Arthurdale to provide community services and support.

She also was an advocate for women and particularly African-Americans in the administration. She wrote a newspaper column, *My Day,* and broke new ground as a First Lady holding press conferences just for women reporters. This idea had first been proposed to her by Lorena Hickok, a reporter who covered her in the White House and then vacationed with her and became one of her closest friends. She worked with Molly Dewson, head of the women's division of the Democratic Party to endorse the hiring of female candidates for government positions.

She would be told by dissatisfied African American leaders of discrimination in the government assistance and programs of the New Deal. When money reached the local level it was in the hands of segregationist leaders in the south and other parts of the country and the money did not benefit African Americans. She would take those complaints to the President and the agencies administering them. She really was the most prominent white person of influence who advocated for civil rights.

In the 1930s she was in close cooperation with the NAACP and its leadership and served on its board. She became a friend and ally of the influential Mary McLeod Bethune who founded the college that became Bethune-Cookman. She persisted in her efforts to get her husband to support an anti-lynching bill in Congress. She set up a meeting with FDR and NAACP President Walter White. FDR would not go along because Southern Democrats were powerful as committee chairpersons in the Congress and he needed them to pass his entire agenda in Congress. When the anti-lynching bill was to be considered in the Senate, Eleanor spent several days sitting in the Senate gallery, clearly wanting her presence to be noted.

She was bold in challenging segregation and racism directly. Invited to speak in Birmingham, Alabama at a conference for Southern progressives in 1938, Public Safety Commissioner Bull Connor said the crowd of 1500 had to be segregated. Eleanor Roosevelt was tapped on the shoulder after she quietly chose to disregard the order and sit in the Black section. She inched her chair into the middle of the aisle between Whites and African Americans and stayed there. (In 1963 Connor infamously unleashed hoses and police dogs on African Americans during civil rights protests in Birmingham).

She created a national stir in 1939 when she resigned from the Daughters of the American Revolution (DAR) because they refused to allow African American singer Marian Anderson to perform a concert in their Constitution Hall. Eleanor then worked with her ally, Interior Secretary Harold Ickes who shared her concern about equal rights, to stage a concert with Anderson at the Lincoln Memorial that was attended by 75,000 people.

Eleanor keenly felt that segregation in the United States undercut its democratic ideals as it was fighting a war against totalitarian countries.

In 1941 A Philip Randolph the President of the Pullman Railroad union became impatient with Roosevelt's unwillingness to integrate the workforce at defense industries and in the military. He decided to call for a massive March on Washington, hoping for 100,000 people to show up. Eleanor arranged for him to meet FDR and directly present his concerns. After listening, FDR agreed and executive order 8022 was developed and signed by the President which banned hiring discrimination and the march was called off.

By establishing a Fair Employment Council with the ability to receive and investigate complaints, it was the first institutionalized process to undo the Jim Crow practices in the federal government. The total de-segregation of the military forces did not happen though until 1948 through an executive order signed by President Truman.

Eleanor who loved flying even made a much publicized flight and media sensation in a Piper Cub with Alfred Anderson of the Tuskegee Airmen.

During the war, FDR approved her going to the South Pacific to see the troops. She visited Australia and was given a reception similar to those given to visiting British royals years earlier.

## The Roosevelt Political Coalition and the Enduring New Deal

The popularity of New Deal programs especially Social Security and the National Labor Relations Act and relief and employment programs like the CCC and WPA earned FDR broad support especially among older persons, organized labor and the unemployed. His steps to appoint some African Americans to federal positions helped him to win African American support which had since Lincoln favored Republicans. He was in a commanding political position not only because of his policies but the personal connection he had made to voters. His 1936 re-election campaign was the first election campaign he would run without Louis Howe who had been his chief political strategist since his first days in Albany. Howe had been in poor health and died while living in the White House where his memorial service was held.

In the campaign, FDR had moved to the left with a withering political attack against "economic royalists" as he accepted re-nomination for a second term at the Democratic National Convention in Philadelphia in June 1936. He gave a soaring speech with biblical undertones about the importance of the battle for a decent life for all people that included not only human rights but economic rights. In the most memorable line, he said,

"There is a mysterious cycle in human events. To some generations much is given. Of other generations much is expected. This generation of Americans has a rendezvous with destiny..... We are poor indeed if this nation cannot afford to lift from every recess of American life the dread fear of the unemployed that they are not needed in the world. We cannot afford to accumulate a deficit in the books of human fortitude. In the place of the palace of privilege we seek to build a temple out of faith and hope and charity."

As he concluded his speech he made a great plea not only for economic support for those in need but also for democracy as Hitler was threatening world peace and totalitarianism was spreading,

"In this world of ours in other lands, there are some people, who, in times past, have lived and fought for freedom, and seem to have grown too weary to carry on the fight. They have sold their heritage of freedom for the illusion of a living. They have yielded their democracy. I believe in my heart that only our success can stir their ancient hope. They begin to know that here in America we are waging a great and successful war. It is not alone a war against want and destitution and economic demoralization. It is more than that; it is a war for the survival of democracy. We are fighting to save a great and precious form of government for ourselves and for the world."

Some Republicans were pushing for Theodore Roosevelt Jr. to be the Republican nominee against his cousin. While FDR was Governor of New York, President Herbert Hoover had appointed TR Jr. to the position of Governor of Puerto Rico and later to be Governor-General of the Philippines. The GOP nominated the moderate Governor of Kansas Alf Landon though who was a progressive in the mold of Teddy Roosevelt.

FDR spoke at the 1936 State Democratic convention in Syracuse which re-nominated Governor Herbert Lehman. In his speech he took aim at the fear mongers who were attacking him. In his customary fashion, he delivered a stinging indictment of their attempt to tie him to Soviet style communism and he linked it to a long line of political smears going back to the founding of the country:

> "There will be - there are - many false issues. In that respect, this will be no different than other campaigns. Partisans, not willing to face realities, will drag out red herrings as they have always done to divert attention from the trail of their own weaknesses. This practice is as old as our democracy. Avoid the facts - fearful of the truth - a malicious opposition charged that George Washington planned to make himself king under a British form of government, that Thomas Jefferson planned to set up a guillotine under a French form of government, that Andrew Jackson soaked the rich of the eastern seaboard and planned to surrender American democracy to the dictatorship of a frontier mob; They called Abraham Lincoln a Roman emperor; Theodore Roosevelt a Destroyer; Woodrow Wilson, a self-constituted Messiah.
>
> In this campaign another herring turns up. This year it is Russian. Desperate in mood, angry at failure, cunning in purpose individuals and groups are seeking to make communism an issue where communism is not a major controversy between the two major parties."

Landon was no match for FDR who won re-election by the largest margin in American history, winning 46 of the 48 states. He lost only Vermont and Maine, gaining 523 electoral votes to 8 for Landon. He won by over 11 million votes with 61% of the vote. The left wing Union Party of Long and Coughlin supporters which had hoped at one time to have the balance or power and get 20% of the vote ended up with 882,000 votes nationwide.

Roosevelt's re-election solidified the coalition that came together to elect him in 1932. He was the first Democrat to win the Black vote and with the support of labor, immigrants and older voters, he had assembled a coalition that would endure and maintain control of the White House for twenty years. It remained the dominant coalition in the party through the late 1960s and the Vietnam War.

In his second term, Roosevelt again invoked the need for the government to stand on the side of those in need. In his second inaugural address in 1937 he famously said, "The test of our progress is not whether we add more to the abundance of those who have much; it is whether we provide enough for those who have too little."

There has been much debate about the impact of Roosevelt's economic policies. There is no question they helped restore confidence and put people to work. Many argue that they made a difference but it was the crisis mobilization of World War II that ended the Great Depression. In fact in Roosevelt's second term, the economy dipped again and he lost his liberal majority in Congress after sustaining major losses in the 1938 midterm elections. His attempt to add seats to the Supreme Court also was unpopular in that period before the midterms elections.

In 1940 FDR was thinking of retiring to a life in the country at Hyde Park. He was worried about who the Democrats would have to replace him. He felt he had no strong progressive successor in the Democratic Party to lead the country in 1940 at such a precarious time. He was sensitive to the precedent it would establish if he ran for a third term since no President had ever done so. He refused to say he was running right up to the Democratic convention and then he orchestrated a draft and floor demonstration which led to his nomination for a third term. The convention was still in an uproar over his choice of Henry Wallace as his new Vice Presidential running mate to replace John Nance Garner. Roosevelt said he would not run if

Wallace was not approved. Eleanor did not want to be involved at the convention but she was dispatched to make a dramatic convention speech - the first by a First Lady - and it helped unite the convention for Wallace's nomination. She received a thunderous ovation and gave a grand, short speech,

> We people in the United States have got to realize today that we face now a grave, a serious situation. Therefore, this year, the candidate who is the President of the United States cannot make a campaign in the usual sense of the word. He must be on his job. So each and every one of you who give him this responsibility, because you will make the campaign, you will have to rise above considerations which are narrow and partisan. You must know that this is the time when all good men and women give every bit of service and strength to their country that they have to give. This is a time when it is the United States that we fight for. The domestic policies that we have established as a party, that we must believe in, that we must carry forward, and in the world we have a position of great responsibility. We cannot tell from day to day what may come.

> This is no ordinary time. No time for weighing anything, except what we can best do for the country as a whole. And that rests, that responsibility on each and every one of us as individuals. No man who is a candidate, or who is president, can carry this situation alone. This is only carried by a united people who love their country and who will live for it to the fullest of their ability with the highest ideals, with the determination that their party shall be absolutely devoted to the good of the nation as a whole and to doing what this country can to bring the world to a safer and happier condition.

FDR went on to defeat Indiana Senator Wendell Willkie by a margin of 5 million votes, 55%-45% while winning 38 states.

## The War Years: Fighting for Democracy and Human Rights

In the late 1930s, war clouds threatened in Europe as Adolf Hitler kept re-arming and sending German troops into Austria and the Sudetenland in Czechoslovakia. While Franklin Roosevelt was a champion of domestic social insurance and economic relief, it was his leadership in World War II and the fight for democracy for which he is also remembered. Nazi Germany and its allies in Italy and Japan threatened to conquer all of Europe and large areas in Africa and Asia, leaving the United States alone defending democracy. A strong isolationist movement in the country with strong memories of World War I had pushed the passage of Neutrality Acts. These policies boxed in Roosevelt's ability to help Great Britain and the democracies in Europe.

As the Nazi military juggernaut conquered most of continental Europe, Roosevelt sought creative ways to aid Great Britain as London and other major cities were bombed during the Blitz to soften it up for an invasion. Roosevelt was able to get Congress to pass the Lend Lease Act to provide old destroyers for Britain in exchange for American access to British military bases.

FDR also wanted to build public support for Great Britain so he invited King George VI and Queen Elizabeth to visit him at Hyde Park for the first royal visit ever to the United States. From May 12-June 17, 1939 the King and Queen were on a five week tour of Canada and they included a five day visit to the United States as part of their trip. They crossed into the United States from Canada at Niagara Falls and traveled through New York State's Southern Tier on the Royal Train to Washington and Mt. Vernon, Virginia. The train then took them to New York where they visited the 1939 World's Fair and traveled up the Hudson River and joined the Roosevelts at Hyde Park. They went to a Sunday church service and were guests at the Roosevelt estate for a hot dog party in the afternoon.

After a long and happy day, they boarded the train again at Hyde Park and through the stormy night they made they way up the Hudson Valley past Albany and Rensselaer where small groups of people were waiting for a glimpse of the royal couple, but they had gone to bed. Storms raged through the North Country and the Adirondacks before they arrived back in Canada the next morning. Just ten weeks later, Hitler invaded Poland and Britain and France declared war to start World War II on September 1, 1939.

Hyde Park was also the setting for many other historic meetings with royalty during the war. Roosevelt was proud of his own Dutch heritage and the history of Dutch settlements in New York. During World War II he offered support for the Dutch monarchy which was in exile after the Netherlands was quickly conquered by the Nazis. Members of the Dutch royal family spent time as guests of the Roosevelts at Hyde Park and in Washington.

In 1940 FDR wrote to Queen Wilhelmina, "I am thinking much of you and the House of Orange in these critical days, and it occurs to me that in the event of the invasion of Holland you may care to have the Crown Princess and the children come to the United States temporarily to be completely safe against airplane raids. It would give Mrs. Roosevelt and me very great happiness to care for them over here as if they were members of our own family and they could come to us either in Washington or at our country place at Hyde Park."

The Queen had hoped to stay in Holland but took a boat to England. She stayed there but visited Canada where her daughter, Crown Princess Juliana was living. In the summer of 1942, they vacationed at Lee, Massachusetts in the Berkshires and the Queen made a visit to Albany to mark the 300th anniversary of the First Church of Albany which was a Dutch Reformed Church. She went on to New York City and then became the first monarch ever to address Congress. Granddaughter, future Queen Beatrix, became a favorite of Franklin and Eleanor Roosevelt. Staying in Massachusetts they made the short visit to Hyde Park. Beatrix would remain in contact with Eleanor and visit her again at Hyde Park on two occasions after her husband's death.

Other royals in exile made stops at Hyde Park and Washington to be with the Roosevelts. Norway was one of the first countries the Nazis conquered and Crown Princess Martha who had visited the United States before the war was invited by FDR to Washington for her safety. She was able to influence Roosevelt to provide support for her country. She spent periods of time at the White House with her children including the current King of Norway, Harald. Martha was one of several women Roosevelt loved to have around him and she attended many social events and some diplomatic ones including traveling with Roosevelt to meet Churchill in Quebec in 1943 when the Atlantic Charter was developed.

Crown Prince Fredrick and Crown Princess Ingrid of Denmark also visited the United States in 1939 and visited the world's fair. The royal family of Luxembourg also were visitors to the United States in 1939.

Everything changed for Roosevelt and the United States on December 7, 1941 when the Japanese attacked Pearl Harbor. Roosevelt gave his famous "Day of Infamy" address to Congress declaring war on Japan and declarations against Germany and Italy followed. After the attack on Pearl Harbor, Roosevelt led a national effort to be the "arsenal of democracy," to build the machinery and weapons to win the war.

When he spoke to Congress on December 8, he wore a black silk armband on his suitcoat because in September he lost his mother Sara who died peacefully at Hyde Park at the age of 86 after months of failing health. She had a simple family funeral at St. James Church and the oldest employees of the Roosevelt estate were pallbearers. The President's children and spouses were there with Eleanor and his mother's brother and sister. Sara was the woman who provided the encouragement and support for his career and political success.

Soon after the Pearl Harbor attack and the United States entry into the war Winston Churchill spent the Christmas season at the White House and then visited Hyde Park during his long stay in the winter of 1941-1942. Eleanor Roosevelt went to Britain in 1942 and was welcomed by the King and Queen. Her trip was a morale booster for the British people and to American soldiers as she visited them in hospitals and military locations.

## The Four Freedoms

Roosevelt's progressive agenda may have started in New York with his bold economic measures to counter the Great Depression. His legacy though also included a firm and moralistic belief in democracy as a statement about the importance of every person's role as a citizen in society. In a war against totalitarianism that produced concentration camps and mass atrocities, Roosevelt constantly invoked the importance of individual freedom and liberty.

One of his greatest speeches and proclamations of human rights occurred with his address to Congress in January 1941 when he articulated what was at stake and what America and its allies were fighting for. He worked hard drafting his speeches, trying to find the right words to express his purpose. He drafted the Four Freedoms - Freedom of Speech, Freedom of Religion, Freedom from Want and Freedom from Fear - to articulate the differences between what democratic nations were fighting to preserve against the totalitarian regimes of Nazi Germany, Italy and Japan.

He launched a public campaign, enlisting the support of artists including Norman Rockwell who produced posters to support the campaign. Rockwell agonized over the how to paint the great concepts of the Four Freedoms and finally decided that he wanted to depict what they meant in simple illustrations of the American people at home, at the dinner table, in church and public meetings.

## *The Second New Deal - Economic Bill of Rights*

As World War II ground forward toward D Day and eventual victory, Franklin Roosevelt envisioned a new agenda after the war and the Great Depression. While the Bill of Rights was the cornerstone of American democracy's individual rights, he felt a "second bill of rights" was needed to guarantee economic freedom for all persons. In his State of the Union address in January 1944, he spelled out in general terms his vision:

> "It is our duty now to begin to lay the plans and determine the strategy for the winning of a lasting peace and the establishment of an American standard of living higher than ever before known. We cannot be content, no matter how high that general standard of living may be, if some fraction of our people—whether it be one-third or one-fifth or one-tenth—is ill-fed, ill-clothed, ill-housed, and insecure.

He made a direct connection between freedom, democracy and a decent standard of living for all, arguing that poverty and economic security were the conditions that made conflict and autocracy likely, "We have come to a clear realization of the fact that true individual freedom cannot exist without economic security and independence.... People who are hungry and out of a job are the stuff of which dictatorships are made.

In our day these economic truths have become accepted as self-evident. We have accepted, so to speak, a second Bill of Rights under which a new basis of security and prosperity can be established for all—regardless of station, race, or creed."

Among these are:

- The right to a useful and remunerative job in the industries or shops or farms or mines of the nation;
- The right to earn enough to provide adequate food and clothing and recreation;
- The right of every farmer to raise and sell his products at a return which will give him and his family a decent living;
- The right of every businessman, large and small, to trade in an atmosphere of freedom from unfair competition and domination by monopolies at home or abroad;
- The right of every family to a decent home;
- The right to adequate medical care and the opportunity to achieve and enjoy good health;
- The right to adequate protection from the economic fears of old age, sickness, accident, and unemployment;
- The right to a good education.

He concluded: "All of these rights spell security. And after this war is won we must be prepared to move forward, in the implementation of these rights, to new goals of human happiness and well-being. America's own rightful place in the world depends in large part upon how fully these and similar rights have been carried into practice for all our citizens. For unless there is security here at home there cannot be lasting peace in the world."

This address seemed to enunciate in one statement the policies and beliefs that Roosevelt had pursued throughout his political career starting in Albany. While some progress has been made on some of the eight points he articulated specifically for medical care and Social Security, rights regarding jobs and housing have not been fulfilled.

## End of the Era

On June 6, 1944, Allied forces made the historic D Day landing in France and the war was in its final year. General Theodore Roosevelt Jr. landed with the troops at Utah Beach in Normandy and a few days later he died of a heart attack.

As World War II moved into this critical phase in 1944, Franklin Roosevelt ran for a fourth term. He was nominated again by the Democratic Party at its convention in Chicago in July though he was traveling to meet General Douglas MacArthur and did not attend the convention. The incumbent Vice President Henry Wallace was replaced by Senator Harry Truman of Missouri as a compromise with conservative Democrats who opposed Wallace. Unwilling to change leaders in the wartime, Roosevelt was elected to a fourth term in 1944 and defeated another New York Governor Thomas E. Dewey.

Roosevelt went to Yalta in early 1945 and met with Churchill and Stalin to make plans for winning the war and planning the post war world.

At the start of his fourth term though his health began to seriously deteriorate. He died on April 12, 1945 in Warm Springs, Georgia at the age of 63 just three weeks before Germany was defeated to end World War II in Europe and five months before the war ended in Japan. His cousin Daisy Suckley was with him and so was Lucy Mercer, the woman he had always loved. His daughter Anna was there but Eleanor was not.

FDR was buried at his family estate at Hyde Park which became the site of the first Presidential library and museum. The funeral train made its way from Washington to Hyde Park where leaders from around the world came to pay respects. All along the way, people cried. He had been to many a father figure who they could personally relate to.

The war was won in August with the Japanese surrender after two atomic bombs were dropped on Hiroshima and Nagasaki. In less than a year, the era of Franklin Roosevelt was over and the postwar world began with a new President.

## FDR in Retrospect

Over the years, Franklin Roosevelt consistently is rated as one of the top three Presidents in American history. He remains at that lofty level even though his legacy has also been re-assessed and he has been criticized for not doing enough to protect ethnic and racial minorities. He has been criticized for not being responsive enough to promote civil rights and to support the anti-lynching bill. Though he personally was opposed to discrimination against any person, civil rights was not a burning political issue for him or the country in the 1930s and 1940s. He did not ban discrimination in the military. It wasn't banned until Harry Truman signed an executive order in 1948.

Roosevelt also has been criticized for not doing enough to accept Jewish refugees during World War II. Both situations need to be put in context though. Discrimination against Jews and African Americans was widespread in the era Roosevelt was President. The criticisms of course are made in historical hindsight. He could have done more but he clearly was not a harsh segregationist or anti-Semite. He took some actions to accept some Jewish refugees. Eleanor lobbied him constantly and he would take actions he felt he could.

The decision that he has been most criticized for and which has left the biggest blemish on his record as President was the forced relocation of 120,000 Japanese Americans on the West Coast after Pearl Harbor. Again, this decision looks worse in time as discrimination that targeted one group because of war hysteria of a possible Japanese invasion on the west coast. Some actions were also taken against Italians and Germans though not on the scale of the re-location of the Japanese. With the approval of her husband, Eleanor Roosevelt visited a Japanese American internment camp at Gila River, Arizona in 1943 and called for them to be closed as soon as possible. They were closed in 1945. In 1976 President Gerald Ford repealed FDR's executive order and in 1988 Congress apologized and authorized reparations of $20,000 for each of 80,000 Japanese Americans.

While FDR had his faults, what is most striking in assessing his career is that he had a remarkable sense of self confidence and he projected an upbeat, positive outlook when the country needed it during the Great Depression. When he said in his 1933 inaugural address, "the only thing we have to fear is fear itself," he was also expressing his own philosophy of life about positive thinking.

One of the best assessments of Franklin Roosevelt was from historian Kenneth Davis, "The image he projected of himself ... continued to be an accurate if partial reflection in the public of what he inwardly was: warm, kind, zestful, joyous, incredibly even-tempered under stress, eager for new experience, interested in everything - a man who, liking everybody, wanted everybody to like him and was exceptionally well equipped to ensure their doing so."

Eleanor, who knew him the best, saw him in much the same way, "While Franklin's desire to make life happier for people was paramount, mixed with it...was his liking for the mechanics of politics, for politics as a science and as a game which included understanding the mass reactions of people and gambling on one's own judgment. Always in Franklin there was evident a sense of humor, which could turn the most serious subject into an object of fun at times when he thought those around him needed a little break in the tension or perhaps a reminder that they were not so important as they thought."

He was a religious man with empathy for the common man and persons in need. Eleanor Roosevelt credited his religious views for his outlook on life and politics. "I always felt that my husband's religion had something to do with his confidence in himself. As I've said, it was a very simple religion. He believed in God and in his guidance. He felt that human beings were given tasks to perform and with those tasks the ability and strength to put them through. He could pray for help in guidance and have faith in his own judgment as a result."

She knew he was a steady man with confidence in himself, the American people and the democratic system of government. She saw his ability to figure out how to make government responsive to peoples' needs.

He had a deep faith in the idea of American democracy and the ability of citizens to be self-governing. He believed though that the "practice" of self governing required a public which was educated about the process and issues of governance and he used the new medium of radio to do that and to enhance prospects for the success of his proposals. He put all of his attributes and political skills in practice as he led the nation through the Great Depression and World War II which were its greatest crises since the Civil War.

# CHAPTER 7

## *Eleanor, The United Nations, Civil Rights, Progressive Champion*

FRANKLIN ROOSEVELT HAD LOOKED FORWARD to the end of the war and creation of the United Nations as an instrument to promote world peace. He had planned to go to San Francisco for the meeting to adopt the charter but it was President Truman who attended in June 1945. FDR also looked forward to going to Great Britain and joining with Churchill to celebrate the victory of the democratic Allies.

After FDR's death, Eleanor Roosevelt returned to New York where she lived her last seventeen years. In March 1946, Winston Churchill who had been voted out in a post war election came to Hyde Park with his wife, Clementine, and daughter, Sarah, to pay their respects at FDR's gravesite. Churchill placed a wreath of white carnations and rhododendron leaves on the grave. He and his family were guests for lunch at Eleanor's Val Kill home. Churchill then made the short trip by car to Albany, visited Governor Thomas E. Dewey and spent the night at the Executive Mansion. Churchill had been pleased with Dewey's support of the British-American alliance during the war and looked forward to meeting him.

Out of the White House, Eleanor was able to pursue causes and issues that were important to her, unrestrained by being the First Lady. She wanted also though to honor and support the legacy of her husband's political life. She wanted to continue to speak for her husband's priorities including the United Nations. President Truman chose Eleanor to be a member of the United States delegation at the first UN meeting in London. Truman called her "The First Lady of the World."

The promotion of human rights was not one of the original goals of the UN. It was decided though to form a human rights commission as part of the Economic and Social Council in the UN structure. The commission would make recommendations on an international standard of human rights. The commission included representatives from Norway, France, Belgium, Peru, China, India, Yugoslavia in addition to Mrs. Roosevelt representing the United States.

The Commission on Human Rights met for the first time on January 27, 1947 in Lake Success, New York, the temporary home of the UN. At its first meeting Eleanor was unanimously elected as the chairperson. The commission spent months in long, tedious discussions and debates and Eleanor made them work so hard that one member quipped that they should have human rights too! The Soviets wanted to add economic rights to be included as human rights. They scoffed at the idea which became the first article of the Declaration of Universal Human Rights, "All human beings are born free and equal in dignity and rights. They are endowed with reason and conscience and should act towards one another in a spirit of brotherhood."

Eleanor Roosevelt had the difficult task as an American advocating for these human rights for all countries while trying to deflect the barbs from other countries that the United States didn't practice human rights with its racist segregation policies in southern states. She also knew southern segregation politicians would not be happy with a human rights declaration that extended those rights to African Americans. The State Department also had top leaders including Undersecretary of State Robert Lovett who felt that economic and social rights did not belong in the Declaration from the United Nations. However, Eleanor persisted and the State Department finally agreed to support her position.

The final document had 30 articles which spelled out many human rights but also included many of the economic rights that Franklin Roosevelt had discussed in his second bill of rights including a reference to social security in a generic sense. When the document was finally approved unanimously 48-0 in Paris on December 10, 1948, Eleanor Roosevelt received a standing ovation on its passage. She said, "It may well become the international Magna Carta for all men everywhere."

She visited Holland that year and was re-united with Princess Juliana and received an honorary degree of Doctor of Laws from the University of Utrecht, the first woman ever given the honor. She said in her newspaper column, "Naturally, the honor bestowed on me is a symbol of Dutch gratitude for the help given by Americans and, particularly, is in recognition of my husband's interest in and concern for Holland, the land of his ancestors. It makes one feel very humble to be the recipient of so much goodwill that comes almost entirely from what others have done."

Eleanor also helped to found the progressive activist organization, Americans for Democratic Action (ADA) in 1947. Her co-founder, Joseph Rauh, Jr., recalled her years later, "Mrs. Roosevelt was a civil rights activist before Martin Luther King Jr. was born, a feminist before the women's liberation movement was conceived, and a determined voice for liberalism in areas that had never seen or heard the likes of her. She will always remain for me the living symbol that one human being--idealistic, unyielding, tireless--can make a difference in improving the lot of one's fellows."

Eleanor traveled and made speeches around the nation and visited many countries, notably India and the Soviet Union. She continued to write her *My Day* newspaper column several times a week. Eleanor showed up on college campuses and even made a celebrity appearance on the "What's My Line?" television show in 1954.

Eleanor remained active in national Democratic party politics as well as in New York State politics. She chaired the Democratic state convention in 1946 in Syracuse when many political leaders in the party wanted her to run for the Senate. In 1948, many wanted her to run for President or be the Vice Presidential nominee on President Truman's ticket in that year when progressive and southern segregationist Democrats defected and ran on separate tickets. She always adamantly refused to run for office, citing her international work at the United Nations and the political activity of her sons. Franklin Jr and James, were both planning their political careers with runs for Congress. James was the Democratic nominee for Governor of California in 1950 but lost to Earl Warren.

Eleanor worked with reformers against the continuing power of Tammany Hall. She had never forgotten the effort of Tammany leader Carmine DiSapio to thwart the bid of her son Franklin Jr in 1954 to be the Democratic nominee for Governor of New York. DiSapio pressured him to step aside for Averell Harriman who won the nomination and was elected Governor. Eleanor worked with reformers to finally end DiSapio's reign in the New York City Democratic Party.

Eleanor identified with the progressive wing of the party that championed civil rights in those years when southern segregationist Democrats still had power as committee chairs in Congress. She was a supporter of Harry Truman in 1948 and then she was a key supporter of Illinois Governor Adlai Stevenson in his two bids for the Presidency in 1952 and 1956.

She was not afraid of Joseph McCarthy and his Communist witch-hunt either and was outspoken against him. In August 1953, she wrote about her trip to Europe in her *My Day* column,

"When I reached Europe I found that there, too, people were more conscious of the methods which had been used by Hitler and Stalin in coming to power, and they invariably felt that Senator McCarthy's methods were identical with those that they had watched successfully enslave many people. We in this country have not had this experience, so it seems impossible to us that anyone should really control our thoughts and actions. But the European people think it quite possible because they have had the experience. For, remember, if the United States should find itself saddled with a dictator there would be no hope of freedom for other parts of the world. The United States has symbolized for the world freedom of thought and action ever since its inception."

She remained active in progressive causes and human and civil rights issues. She met Rosa Parks and a young Martin Luther King, Jr. after he had led the Montgomery bus boycott in 1955. She worked on the party platform in 1956 that would embrace the Brown vs. Board of Education Supreme Court ruling outlawing segregation in public schools. In New York, she worked with Jackie Robinson who became a civil rights activist after retiring from baseball.

She kept a busy travel schedule campaigning for Adlai Stevenson's presidential run. She had supported his candidacy over New York Governor Averell Harriman who she had known since he was a child. She thought they were good leaders but realized as years went on how great a politician and leader her husband had been. People were realizing too that she was a great power in her own right. She was considered the Democrats' best surrogate to speak for its candidates.

She had become close friends with her doctor, David Gurewitsch, and she ended up buying a home with him in New York and even remained when he married his wife Edna. Eleanor also continued to live at Hyde Park too and loved to meet with groups of young people. In July 1955, she met with an Elizabeth, New Jersey Jewish youth group which had written her asking if she would meet with them on their two day tour that stopped first at West Point and then went to Hyde Park. She agreed and said she would meet them at FDR's favorite oak tree. Beatrice and Don Cohen led the group and Bea wrote, "Arriving at Hyde Park, a young lady from the Roosevelt Library led us to the spacious lawn. There stood the greatest First Lady under FDR's favorite oak tree, both standing tall - and strong and sturdy. Above her, the tree's lush green leaves formed a protective umbrella. When we approached, she welcomed us warmly, her hands clasped behind her, she was wearing a soft blue and white dress, her gray hair piled high framed a kind and gentle face. She told of the President's childhood and boyhood growing up in this, his beloved Hyde Park home.

She predicted that air travel would be accelerated in the 21st century, we would be able to travel from New York to Africa in 4 or 5 hours. The world was getting smaller, that America was a global power with global responsibilities.

'Will we ever have a woman President,' I asked. "Yes, she said, when there are more women in government, local, state and national."

In 1959 she was visited by the new Soviet Premier Nikita Khrushchev. He was visiting the United Nations and then made the 78 mile trip to Hyde Park. That same month, one of Eleanor's young favorites, Princess Beatrix, paid a visit while she was in the United States to mark the 350th anniversary of Henry Hudson's exploration in New York.

In 1960 Eleanor did not feel that Senator John F. Kennedy had enough experience to lead the nation and that he would not vigorously pursue civil rights legislation that was of paramount importance to her. She had a distant relationship with Kennedy's father, Joseph, who she thought was trying to buy the nomination for his son. She also remembered how he was a defeatist as FDR's Ambassador to Great Britain during the war and that the Kennedy family had a friendly, personal relationship with Joseph McCarthy.

She supported a failed effort to get Adlai Stevenson to run again for the nomination. She had met with state delegations and was urging Kennedy to be the Vice Presidential candidate with Stevenson. When Kennedy won the nomination, he met with Eleanor at Hyde Park and she supported him in the fall campaign. Kennedy asked her how he could win her full support and she said by appointing Stevenson as Secretary of State. After he was elected, Kennedy didn't do that but he appointed Stevenson to be Ambassador to the United Nations, a key post in the Cold War where he memorably confronted the Soviets publicly during the Cuban Missile Crisis.

Eleanor attended the inauguration of President Kennedy on January 20, 1961. She refused to sit on the podium though, choosing to sit below in public seating. She was glad to see a young family with children back in the White House. She and Kennedy exchanged communications and she offered her opinions on public issues he faced. Kennedy appointed her to chair the Committee on the Status of Women. He appointed her back to the UN delegation. In January 1961, weeks before Kennedy's inaugural she wrote an *Atlantic* magazine article of her support for a program like the Peace Corps in the midst of the Cold War and Russian engagement with the Third World:

"If many of our young people have lost the excitement of the early settlers, who had a country to explore and develop, it is because no one remembers to tell them that the world has never been so challenging, so exciting; the fields of adventure and new fields to conquer have never been so limitless. There is still unfinished business at home, but there is the most tremendous adventure in bringing the peoples of the world to an understanding of the American dream."

On March 1, 1961 she interviewed President Kennedy for a radio program about the creation of the Peace Corps which inspired her because of its international voluntarism of American youth. She agreed to serve on the advisory board to the program.

In 1961 in poor health she still managed to chair the commission on justice that was investigating the treatment of the young Freedom Riders who were beaten as they traveled on buses in the South. Jon Meacham in his biography of John Lewis, *His Soul is Marching On*, quoted Eleanor Roosevelt telling her secretary, "I had the most wonderful dream last night. I dreamt I was marching and singing and sitting in with the students in the South."

She persisted even when she no longer had Secret Service protection and there were death threats against her as she set out to speak for integration. The Ku Klux Klan offered a $25,000 reward for anyone who would kidnap her.

Martin Luther King spoke at the annual Roosevelt dinner of the Americans for Democratic Action (ADA) in 1961 and Eleanor was present. She joined the board of the NAACP. She taught at the Highlander school for civil rights activists. She was the first donor giving $100 to the Student Nonviolent Coordinating Committee (SNCC) where John Lewis would become a prominent leader.

She lived long enough to see the revolution in the world against colonialism and the fight for civil rights in the United States. On her last New Year's Day in 1962 she wrote in her My Day column, "The trend in all parts of the world, however, is to do away with second-class people and second-class citizenship, and we are affected in our country by this same world trend. We would be shocked if anyone told us that the position of the Negro in this country seemed in other parts of the world to have some attributes of colonialism. Yet, this is actually the way great areas of the world look upon certain situations in both our North and South. These situations are only accentuated and much more evident in the Southern states.

We are extremely fortunate that our Negro leaders have worked under the spell of the Gandhian philosophy. Martin Luther King presses forward but he presses forward without the use of violence and with the constant hope that there will be love and understanding growing out of each new gain. Passive resistance is used to oppose what our colored citizens consider injustice and inequality, which they will no longer tolerate."

Eleanor Roosevelt remained active even as her health declined. At the height of the Cold War, she made her last public appearance in Albany at the State University on October 19, 1961 to speak at a forum on the topic, "How the United States Can Best Influence the World Against Communism."

In 1962 she became ill and weaker. In her last public effort she wrote a letter to President Kennedy urging him to order the desegregation of public housing.

She died on election day, November 7, 1962 at the age of 78 at her Val-Kill cottage, exactly 30 years after the election of 1932 sent her and Franklin to the White House. She was laid to rest next to her husband. Her funeral was attended by Presidents Kennedy, Eisenhower and Truman and Vice President Lyndon Johnson who became President the following year. She had been born in the 19th century during the administration of Grover Cleveland and she lived to see John F. Kennedy become President.

Kennedy had been smitten by her and nominated her posthumously for the Nobel Peace Prize. He issued a statement saying, "Our condolences go to all the members of her family, whose grief at the death of this extraordinary woman can be tempered by the knowledge that her memory and spirit will long endure among those who labor for great causes around the world."

In his eulogy at Hyde Park, Adlai Stevenson said, "What other single human being has touched and transformed the existence of so many others?"

Paying tribute to her after her death, Martin Luther King said, "The impact of her personality and its unwavering dedication to high principle and purpose cannot be contained in a single day or era...Her life was one of the bright interludes in the troubled history of mankind."

# CHAPTER 8

## *The Progressive Legacy of Franklin and Eleanor Roosevelt*

**PRESIDENT HARRY TRUMAN** carried on the New Deal with his Fair Deal though he became stymied by the Cold War, McCarthyism and a Republican controlled Congress that tried to rollback some of the New Deal. The New Deal was so popular with the public, especially Social Security, that repeated Republican efforts to repeal or roll it back never got far and most Republicans accepted the permanence of the programs. President Eisenhower, the first Republican after Roosevelt and Truman, supported the expansion of Social Security with an amendment which he signed on August 1, 1956 that created the Social Security Disability Insurance program.

On August 14, 1960, Senator John F. Kennedy of Massachusetts, the young, Presidential nominee of the Democratic Party made the trek to Hyde Park to mark the 25th anniversary of Social Security and to pay a visit to Eleanor Roosevelt after the Democratic convention.

Kennedy used his visit to Hyde Park to laud Social Security and commit himself to complete what FDR wanted with a major expansion of the social welfare for older Americans, "Today we commemorate one of those battles - the passage of the Social Security Act of

1935 - the most important single piece of social welfare legislation in the history of this country."

He also said he wanted to complete what FDR had hoped would be part of Social Security by adding national health insurance. "First, we must enact immediately an adequate, comprehensive plan to enable our older citizens to meet their pressing medical needs. Such a plan, a soundly-financed program - without a destructive, degrading means test - based on the tried and tested operation of the Social Security system, is now before Congress; and it can - and should - and must be enacted this year! "

He advocated for adding a health care program that would become Medicare when it was enacted five years later.

Kennedy added, "This story is a living story, not merely statistics. It is deeply burned into every city and town, every hospital and clinic, every neighborhood and rest-home in America, wherever our older citizens live out their lives in want and despair under the shadow of illness. You have seen it in your state - I have seen it in my travels across all fifty states. It is a sight engraved upon our minds and hearts - but it is a sight which, together, we can wipe from the face of this great rich land forever.

But I also say to you that this bill will be - like the original Social Security law - only a single stone in an unfinished structure. It is an important start toward meeting the health problems of our older citizens - but it is only a start. And the coming years will require even more of us."

Ironically, it was Kennedy's death and the legislative skills of President Lyndon Johnson that led to the passage of many of the programs Kennedy endorsed. Johnson began his political career winning a seat in Congress in 1938 with the endorsement of President Roosevelt. Following the assassination of President John F. Kennedy, Johnson won a landslide victory in 1964. In 1965, he used his majorities and his experience and knowledge of Congress where he served as Senate Majority Leader to enact the most comprehensive series of programs since the New Deal.

Johnson's Great Society launched a new War on Poverty with a new Office of Economic Opportunity (OEO). He also secured passage of the Older Americans Act which established agencies on aging in counties nationwide. Johnson also was able to pass the most significant civil rights and voting rights legislation following sit-ins and marches of the Civil Rights movement.

The American Medical Association again opposed legislation to enact a national health care program for older Americans and a program for the disabled and the poor. However, Johnson was able to fulfill part of the aim of the original Social Security Act by winning passage of the Medicare and Medicaid programs as amendments to the Social Security Act. He signed the legislation on July 30, 1965 in Independence, Missouri, the home of President Harry Truman who attended and was honored for his role in promoting health insurance while in office.

## 50th *anniversary of Social Security*

In the early 1970s during the Nixon Administration, a new program called Supplemental Security Income (SSI) was passed to provide what was regarded as a supplement to Social Security for the aged, blind and disabled who were so poor their Social Security benefit was below a minimal level.

Over the years, Social Security became the "third rail" of American politics but that did not prevent conservative forces from pushing for changes especially when they gained power in the Reagan and Bush years. Reagan had been accused of favoring privatization of Social Security but he never pursued it. He did seek cuts in the program. At the time, the Social Security program passed through a harrowing financial crisis when it was in danger of running out of money. A bipartisan commission was appointed to come up with a rescue plan. Some of the most prominent leaders in Washington served on the Commission which recommended an increase in the payroll tax and other program changes including gradually raising the retirement age from 65 to 67 over several decades. In 1982, Congress faced with the program running out of funding, passed the recommendations of the commission that included enough revenues to sustain the program's Trust Fund into the 21st century.

Sensing the continuing threats to Social Security, a 50th anniversary celebration of the program's passage was attended by an estimated crowd of 5200 older persons and advocates gathered on the front yard of FDR's Springwood home on August 15, 1985. Planning had taken place for months with labor unions and senior organizations and other community groups which were members of a large sponsoring coalition Save Our Security, formed in 1978 to defend the program. To those activists attending, Social Security was a cornerstone of a better older life which they intended to defend during the Reagan years.

Many were union members and warriors in many social justice crusades. They were fiercely loyal to Social Security and ready to fight those who might try to alter its social insurance foundation. Most of the seniors remembered the passage of the bill a half century earlier and they came to celebrate what they viewed as the most important government program ever established.

There are on the steps of Springwood Roosevelt's family home just a few feet from the graves of Eleanor and Franklin Roosevelt the living leaders of the movement for Social Security gathered to celebrate the program. The honorary co-chairmen of the celebration were Franklin

D Roosevelt Jr. and Robert Wagner the former New York City mayor and son of the senator who had sponsored the Social Security Act. New York Governor Mario Cuomo gave the keynote address with other remarks by Congressman Claude Pepper, former Health, Education and Welfare secretary Arthur Fleming.

Cuomo was eloquent as always saying, "For the 50 years since President Franklin Delano Roosevelt signed the Social Security act millions of Americans have known that Social Security works. We have sustained it with contributions from the fruits of our labor, defended it against those who would take it away from people in need and improved it for the security of future generations. FDR knew 50 years ago what we all know now, that Social Security is in the mainstream of the American philosophy of social responsibility and action. FDR once said that the social objectives of his administration were to do what any honest government of any country would do to try to increase the security and happiness of a larger number of people in all occupations of life and in all parts of the country to give them assistance so that they are not going to starve in old age. We still subscribe to those goals today of social responsibility and action."

Cuomo summarized, "Some of us are where we are today, and have affluence, even grandeur because of a change begun a half century ago, because of a government that had a heart and a head. Franklin Roosevelt put in place the cornerstone of a new America."

In 1990 the Americans with Disabilities Act was passed by a Democratic Congress and signed into law by President George H. W. Bush to provide accommodations to disabled persons in workplace and public settings.

President Kennedy's brother, Senator Edward Kennedy introduced legislation and became a Congressional champion for national health care which was never seriously considered during the Reagan-Bush years. President Bill Clinton made a proposal for a national health plan that failed in 1994 and was a factor that cost Democrats control of Congress. In 1996 the Republican Congress repealed the Aid for Families with Dependent Children (AFDC) program, the program which was originally part of the Social Security law.

It was not until 2010 that a program of national health pushed by President Barack Obama was available for all Americans through the Affordable Care Act or Obamacare as it became known. It became a controversial program that was twice upheld by the Supreme Court and the Republican controlled Congress passed legislation numerous times to kill it but the bills were vetoed by Obama.

Supporters and beneficiaries of the program expected it to be repealed in 2017 after Donald Trump was elected President and pledged to do away with the program and replace it with something better. He was unable to do either.

President Joe Biden's first agenda item in 2021 after winning the election during the coronavirus pandemic which crushed the world economy was a $1.9 trillion economic relief measure. This legislation was called the most significant progressive legislation since the New Deal. It included $1400 payments for individuals, expanded unemployment insurance, increases in food assistance, a child care tax credit and support for state and local governments and small businesses. Biden also proposed major environmental legislation to fight climate change. Others were urging him to endorse a platform called "The Green New Deal" which proposed to dramatically transition American energy consumption from fossil fuels to clean energy from solar, wind and other sources as well as to promote job creation in clean energy industries. He did propose a Civilian Climate Corps to re-launch the CCC, enrolling young people again to work on environmental projects to address climate change.

## FDR's Progressive Legacy in New York

FDR's Lt. Governor Herbert Lehman succeeded him as Governor in 1933 and he embarked on a Little New Deal in New York that helped address the Great Depression at the state level. He passed a minimum wage law and implemented a stronger old age pension law that included the concept of payroll deductions. He enacted unemployment insurance and a state version of the Wagner Act which allowed unionization. He served for 10 years as Governor, re-elected in 1934, 1936 and then won the state's first four year term in 1938 before resigning in 1942 to become the head of the State Department's Office of Foreign Relief and Rehabilitation Operations. He served in the United States Senate from 1949-1957.

Another person who was a close advisor for FDR in the 1940s and later was elected Governor of New York in 1954 was Averell Harriman. He had made a fortune in the Union Pacific Railroad. Harriman had served as Ambassador to the Soviet Union and was a key foreign policy aide who married Winston Churchill's daughter, Pamela. Harriman promoted progressive programs in consumer protection, public housing and civil rights. He also launched anti-poverty programs that were a forerunner for those nationally promoted a decade later by Lyndon Johnson. Harriman only served one term, falling in 1958 in an election called the "battle of millionaires" against Republican Nelson Rockefeller. Rockefeller then served fifteen years as Governor until resigning in 1973. He was then appointed as Vice President the following year by President Gerald Ford who became President following Richard Nixon's resignation.

Rockefeller had worked in the federal government in Roosevelt's state department. Roosevelt appointed the 32 year old Rockefeller in 1940 to the new post of coordinator of the Office of Inter-American Affairs. In 1944, Rockefeller became assistant secretary of state for American affairs. He played a key role in hemisphere policy at the

United Nations Conference held in San Francisco, developing consensus for regional pacts. Although Roosevelt tried to convince Rockefeller to become a Democrat, he remained a Republican as were his family members.

As Governor, Rockefeller was a progressive who was a champion of civil rights. He made significant contributions to civil rights organizations and was trusted by key leaders. In New York, he was known as an activist governor who spent big on public projects including building the state university of New York system.

During Rockefeller's first year as Governor, the St. Lawrence Seaway finally was completed. It was Canada's decision to build the Seaway and not wait for action by the United States that finally set the stage for passage along with the advent of the Cold War and the important benefits for national security.

President Eisenhower was also a supporter of the Seaway and he signed the Wiley-Dondero Act in 1954 that approved America's partnership with Canada in building the Seaway. Five years later, Queen Elizabeth II and President Eisenhower presided at the opening of the Seaway in Canada on June 26, 1959 and the next day she and Vice President Richard Nixon dedicated the Moses-Saunders power dam near Massena, New York.

Another Democrat, Congressman Hugh Carey, finally won the governor 's office in 1974 in the midst of the Watergate scandal. Carey though entered office in the midst of a fiscal crisis and famously said "the days of wine and roses are over."

Fifty years after Roosevelt left the Governor's mansion, the man in recent history, Mario Cuomo, who was most associated with the Roosevelt values and philosophy was also elected by a small margin. In the midst of the Reagan presidency which sought to turn back the liberal era that began with FDR, Cuomo became the most significant governor and voice who articulated his story of the "Family of New

York." He often cited Roosevelt's philosophy of taking care of those in need and famously gave the keynote address at the 1984 Democratic national convention when he spoke of a tale of two cities, summoning the progressive themes of FDR in responding to the trickle down economics of President Ronald Reagan.

# EPILOGUE

PRESIDENT JOSEPH BIDEN took office in 2021 during the height of the coronavirus pandemic which had decimated the economy as businesses, schools, travel and entertainment closed and unemployment skyrocketed. Many said he took office in the worst crisis since Franklin Roosevelt entered the White House during the Depression. Not only did Biden have to face the crisis of the pandemic, but he faced three other major crises including the economic collapse following the pandemic, heightened racial reckoning following the deaths of George Floyd and others in 2020. Biden also faced a deeply divided nation that needed to unite and address the rise of domestic terrorism and extremism which had culminated two weeks before Biden's inauguration when supporters of President Donald Trump stormed the United States Capitol to try to stop the certification of the election results.

On October 27, 2020 a week before the presidential election, Biden saw an opportunity to win the state of Georgia for the Democrats for the first time since 1992. In the midst of the pandemic he went to Warm Springs, Georgia and FDR's Little White House to campaign and talk about how to heal the nation after the divisiveness of the Trump administration.

In his speech, Biden said, "A few weeks ago, I spoke at Gettysburg about the need to unite our nation, and today I'm here at Warm Springs because I want to talk about how we're going to heal our nation. Over these past few months, there's been so much pain, and so much suffering, and so much loss in America. Over 225,000 people have lost their lives to a virus...."

Biden concluded, "FDR came looking for a cure, but it was the lessons he learned here that he used to lift a nation. Humility, empathy, courage, optimism. This place represented a way forward. A way of restoration, of resilience, of healing. In the years that followed, FDR would come back to Warm Springs often to think about how to heal the nation and the world, and that's exactly what he did. Lifting us out of a great depression, defeating tyranny, saving democracy.

Then it was here on April 12th, 1945, that President Roosevelt died. A casualty of war as surely as any who fell in combat, and the free world mourned. American leaders wept. Maybe even more important was the reaction of the American people. Naval Chief Petty Officer Graham Jackson, a black man, cried as he played his accordion in tribute to FDR, not far from here.

And the story is told that when Franklin Delano Roosevelt's procession went by, a man collapsed in grief. The neighbor asked him, 'Did you know the president?' The response was 'No,' the man said, 'but he knew me.' He knew me. Few words better describe the kind of president our nation needs right now."

# END NOTES

## *Roosevelt Family Legacy*

THE FRANKLIN AND ELEANOR ROOSEVELT Presidential Museum and
Library today is a national historic landmark. The family's Springwood home and the other cottages at Val Kill are all part of the historic
site which welcomes thousands of persons every year. The East 65
Street homes of the Roosevelts are now known as Roosevelt House and
part of Hunter College of the City University of New York. In 1997
the FDR Memorial was completed and dedicated in Washington with
statues of both Franklin and Eleanor. After Eleanor's death, the family
deeded its property at Campobello Island to the governments of the
United States and Canada and it is now the Roosevelt Campobello
International Park. Four Freedoms Park is located on Roosevelt Island
in New York City.

The Roosevelt children were active in politics and public life
though not as successful as their father. In February 1963 after her
mother had died, Anna Roosevelt Halstead was appointed by President Kennedy as vice-chairman of the President's Commission for the
Observance of Human Rights. Franklin Jr. served in Congress from
New York from 1949-55. He sought the Democratic nomination for
Governor of New York in 1954 and lost to Averell Harriman. He was

appointed Under Secretary of Commerce by President Kennedy. He later was appointed by President Lyndon Johnson to chair the Equal Employment Opportunity Commission. He ran for Governor of New York on the Liberal Party line in 1966 and was defeated by Governor Nelson Rockefeller.

Another son, James, served as a Congressman from California from 1955-1965, and lost a bid for Governor in 1950. In the 1980s, he founded the National Committee to Preserve Social Security and Medicare which remains a leading advocacy organization. Elliott wrote many books including *The Untold Story* about his parents' lives. John Roosevelt was a businessman who never ran for political office and became a Republican who endorsed President Dwight Eisenhower. All of the children of FDR and Eleanor have passed away.

Some of the grandchildren are very active in public affairs. James Roosevelt III worked for the Social Security Administration and was CEO of the Tufts Health plan. He is co-chair of the bylaws committee of the Democratic National Committee. In 1986 he ran for Congress in a primary that pitted him against Joseph P. Kennedy III who won the seat.

## Key allies, aides

AL SMITH, the man who had promoted FDR to be Governor, passed away just weeks before the presidential election in October 1944. They had been political allies in New York politics but then grew apart as Smith tried to stop Roosevelt in 1932 from winning the Democratic presidential nomination. Smith became a member of the Liberty League that opposed many policies of the New Deal. Though still a Democrat Smith endorsed Republicans Alf Landon for President in 1936 and Wendell Willkie in 1940. In later years though Smith and

FDR had a friendly relationship. Smith appreciated how Roosevelt contacted him when his wife died.

**HARRY HOPKINS** married his third wife and lived in the White House until 1943. He had suffered from stomach cancer and died of related health problems in 1945 at the age of 55.

**FRANCES PERKINS** did not remain as Labor Secretary after FDR's death but was asked by President Truman in 1945 to serve on the Civil Service Commission which she did until 1952. She later taught at the New York State School of Industrial and Labor Relations at Cornell University until her death in 1965 at the age of 85.

**HENRY MORGENTHAU** died in Poughkeepsie in 1967 at the age of 75 and his family still owns Fishkill Farms in Hopewell Junction, New York.

**JAMES FARLEY** was the last surviving member of the FDR Cabinet when he died in 1976 at the age of 88. He had a falling out with Roosevelt after he was no longer national party chair. He was a close political ally of President Harry Truman.

*Eleanor Roosevelt interviewed by Dan Burgess (author's father) at State University, Potsdam, NY May 1955*

# AUTHOR'S NOTES

I WAS NOT ALIVE during the lifetime of Franklin D. Roosevelt. I remember first hearing about Eleanor Roosevelt at age nine when it was reported on election night in 1962 that she had died. Franklin Roosevelt was just a few years older than my two grandfathers and he was the Governor of New York and President during their middle aged years. He was the President during the childhood and adolescence of my parents who were born just before he became Governor and then led the nation through the Great Depression and World War II. He died just as they were becoming adults in April 1945, a month before V-E Day and the end of the war in Europe.

My father, Dan Burgess, had a 1955 photo of him interviewing Mrs. Roosevelt when he was a 29 year old radio announcer for WMSA radio in nearby Massena where we lived when I was born. She was visiting the State University of New York in Potsdam. In her *My Day* newspaper column at the time, she said went to what was then called the Potsdam State Teachers College to see their new library, music and arts programs including some art created by WPA workers in the New Deal.

I learned later of Mrs. Roosevelt's connection to Massena and the North Country region. There was a picture of her standing on the porch on Elm Street. This house was next door to where my aunt and uncle later lived along with two of my uncles on the same block. Eleanor was visiting there at the home of Alfred Cook, the brother of her close friend and collaborator Nancy Cook. Marguerite "Missy" LeHand was FDR's personal secretary and close confidante and her family lived in Potsdam.

I wrote about the Roosevelts in my previous book Keeper of the Olympic Flame when Roosevelt as Governor opened the 1932 Lake Placid Olympics.

In fact, the Roosevelts had an affection for Lake Placid. Over the years, Franklin and Eleanor made numerous trips to the North Country. Franklin's mother Sara vacationed there. In the 1920s, while he was running the Warm Springs, Georgia resort for persons afflicted by polio, FDR had entrepreneurial ambitions and thought about a string of health resorts from Warm Springs to Lake Placid, according to his son, Elliott.

Of course, the legacy of this legendary First Couple was still omnipresent in the America of my childhood in the late 1950s and 1960s. In school, studying American history, I was interested in Roosevelt's New Deal programs and policies that established Social Security and work programs like the Civilian Conservation Corps (CCC) to address unemployment. Later, when I began working in the field of aging and human services, I had a better understanding and appreciation of the impact of the Social Security program. My first book, *To the Last Breath*, was about my friend, the remarkable senior advocate Rose Kryzak, who remembered attending rallies for Social Security in the 1930s. I was with Rose and thousands of other advocates in 1985 when I went to the FDR home, Springwood, and Presidential library and museum in Hyde Park, New York for the 50th anniversary celebration of the Social Security Act.

Twenty years later in 2005, I rode a bus with retired teachers and other union retirees to return to Hyde Park for the 70th anniversary of the program. Five years later in 2010 to mark the 75th anniversary of the program, I presided as Director of the New York State Office for the

Aging at ceremonies in Albany and took part at other events in Hyde Park and at Roosevelt House at Hunter College in New York City.

Through all the years of advocacy with older persons we have had to always be vigilant to protect the program from those who have cut its funding, weaken it or privatize it because they have opposed the concept of government-run social insurance.

My interest in the Roosevelts continued to grow with these visits to Hyde Park and as I learned more about their interesting personal lives during that period of history. I have learned more about their visits with famous people in Hyde Park as well as the many people and places they visited in my native upstate New York.

FDR returned home to New York throughout his presidency. He made many visits across the state for important projects that he began as Governor. Among them, he attended the opening of the Whiteface Mountain Memorial highway in September 1935 and the 50th anniversary of the Conservation Act in New York State in Lake Placid. He also attended the opening of the Thousand Islands Bridge to Canada in 1938, another project he encouraged as Governor.

I have greatly admired Eleanor Roosevelt's history of activism in social issues and causes during her time as First Lady and after the death of her husband when she traveled extensively across the country and throughout the world.

# ACKNOWLEDGMENTS

WRITING A BOOK IS A BIG PERSONAL ENDEAVOR. This book was my pandemic project that I started in 2020. Turning this fun into a book requires help. Meradith Kill at the Troy Book Makers helped to make the book a reality through their publishing assistance to authors with layout, design and production. Marcia Rosen helped with developmental editing and was a sounding board for me who helped me to focus and organize my message in this book. The staff of the New York State Archives assisted me in accessing the correspondence of Franklin Roosevelt as Governor.

I asked three friends who have an interest in the Roosevelts and politics to read a draft of the book and provide feedback. Thanks to Steve Madarasz, Howard Schaeffer and Ruth Smith. My daughter, Catherine and son Joseph, also read parts of the book and gave me suggestions.

Researching and writing this book has been a time of fun as I discovered new, little known vignettes in the daily lives of the Roosevelts. My wife, Kate, has been a great listener as I regaled her with some of the stories I discovered about the life and times of the Roosevelts in Albany and other places many years ago. And she, like I, has become a greater fan of Eleanor Roosevelt as a humanitarian who lived her faith and of Franklin as the easy going politician who projected leadership and confidence when it was most needed.

# BIBLIOGRAPHY

A First Class Temperament, Geoffrey Ward

The Black Cabinet, Jill Watts

CCC Camps in the Adirondacks, Martin Podskoch

Eleanor Roosevelt, Blanche Wiesen Cook

Eleanor in the Village, Jan Jarboe Russell

Eleanor The Years Alone, Joseph Lash

Eleanor and Franklin, Joseph Lash

FDR, The New York Years, 1928-1933, Kenneth Davis

Franklin D. Roosevelt as Governor of New York, Bernard Bellush

Franklin and Winston, Jon Meacham

Freedom from Fear, David Kennedy

The Great Depression, David Watkins

His Truth is Marching On, Jon Meacham

The Lion and The Fox, James McGregor Burns

The Man He Became, James Tobin

No Ordinary Time, Doris Kearns Goodwin

The Roosevelts of Hyde Park, An Untold Story, Elliott Roosevelt

The Train to Crystal City, Jan Jarboe Russell

The Woman Behind the New Deal, Kirstin Downey

New York State Archives, Papers of Governor Roosevelt

Franklin D. Roosevelt Library and Museum, Master Speech Files

New York Times

Albany Times Union

Wikipedia

# INDEX

# ABOUT THE AUTHOR

MICHAEL BURGESS was born in Massena, New York, grew up in Watertown and graduated from St. Lawrence University in Canton. After college he moved to Albany and worked as an advocate for older New Yorkers at the state capital. In 2007, he was appointed the Director of the New York State Office for the Aging by Governor Eliot Spitzer. He was re-appointed to the position when David Paterson became Governor in 2008 and served until November 2010.

This is Michael's fourth book. In 2003 he published, *Rose Kryzak and the Senior Action Movement in New York.* In 2012 he published *A Long Shot to Glory : How Lake Placid Saved the Winter Olympics and Restored the Nation's Pride.* In 2016 he published *Keeper of the Olympic Flame: Lake Placid's Jack Shea vs. Avery Brundage and the Nazi Olympics.*

Michael has also written many newspaper commentaries and magazine articles on public issues and history in New York State which have appeared in Newsday, the *Albany Times Union, Adirondack Life* and the *New York State Archives* magazine.

He currently is a consultant with community organizations in the Albany area and lives in Delmar with his wife Kathleen.

You can reach him by email at *mjburgess1002@gmail.com.*